Making Good Schools

The disciplines of school effectiveness research and school improvement practice and research have been apart for too long. This book is the first major attempt by leading writers and practitioners in these fields to bring the areas together in a coherent way. Existing knowledge about the characteristics of 'good' schools is outlined, together with the knowledge base about how to 'make schools good schools'. The book also makes an entirely original contribution to re-thinking practice in school improvement that can revolutionise our thinking in the late 1990s and which can be of use to academics, policy-makers and practitioners.

David Reynolds is Professor in the Department of Education at the University of Newcastle-upon-Tyne. **Robert Bollen** is Chair of the Foundation for International Collaboration on School Improvement. **Bert Creemers** is Professor at the University of Groningen, the Netherlands. **David Hopkins** is Professor at the University of Nottingham. **Louise Stoll** is a Senior Lecturer at the Institute of Education, University of London. **Nijs Lagerweij** is a Professor at Utrecht University, the Netherlands.

Educational management series
Series editor: Cyril Poster

Making Good Schools

Linking school effectiveness and school improvement

David Reynolds, Robert Bollen, Bert Creemers, David Hopkins, Louise Stoll and Nijs Lagerweij

with the assistance of
Gerard van den Hoven and Boudewijn van Velzen

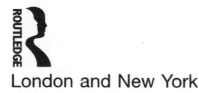

London and New York

First published 1996
by Routledge
11 New Fetter Lane, London EC4P 4EE

Simultaneously published in the USA and Canada
by Routledge
29 West 35th Street, New York, NY 10001

© 1996 David Reynolds, Robert Bollen, Bert Creemers, David
Hopkins, Louise Stoll and Nijs Lagerweij

Typeset in Times by Routledge
Printed and bound in Great Britain by
TJ Press (Padstow) Ltd, Padstow, Cornwall

British Library Cataloguing in Publication Data
A catalogue record for this book is available from the British
Library

Library of Congress Cataloguing in Publication Data
A catalogue record for this book has been requested

ISBN 0–415–13023–9 (hbk)
ISBN 0–415–13024–7 (pbk)

Contents

Illustrations

Foreword

Since the mid-1980s there has been considerable interest in school effectiveness and school improvement among researchers, policy-makers and practitioners. The International Congress for School Effectiveness and School Improvement (ICSEI) has been prominent in these fields, creating an intellectual setting where knowledge can advance through cross-cultural and interdisciplinary collaboration. In this context, the Foundation for International Collaboration on School Improvement (FICSI) decided in the early 1990s to make a contribution to this field of study. School improvement dates back to the mid-1980s as a field of study, and special mention must be made in this context of the International School Improvement Project (ISIP) which established a distinctive body of knowledge that became internationally recognised.

The first activity that FICSI undertook was to organise special symposia at the annual meetings of ICSEI in which individuals from the two distinct fields of 'effectiveness' and 'improvement' presented material that showed where they were intellectually 'coming from'. It was clear from these sessions that the 'effectiveness' people viewed school improvement as operating on a modest empirical base that was weak and eclectic. By contrast, school 'improvement' people expressed surprise about the reluctance of effectiveness researchers to explore interventions within schools.

Nevertheless, dialogue created between representatives of the two paradigms was so productive that a group of people decided to integrate the two bodies of knowledge, beginning with a meeting in Cardiff in summer 1993 and continuing with subsequent meetings. At this stage APS (National Centre for School Improvement, Utrecht, the Netherlands) decided to support this effort, and also the subsequent decision to proceed with the publication of a book that was to outline the results of deliberations as we sought to integrate 'effectiveness' and 'improvement'. APS has been happy to give a considerable amount of secretarial help, staff time and general support, which is needed to make sure that a book like this can see the light of day.

It is clear that the final version of the book, as it emerged after months of work, editing and debate among the authors, may be a first step on the road to integrating effectiveness and improvement rather than a final statement. From the point of view of APS, there need to be further links between the worlds of research and practice, effectiveness and improvement, and policy and practice, in order to meet the needs of teachers and school leaders.

We at APS will seek to build on the useful foundations of this book in order to carry the process further.

Gerard van den Hoven, Director
Boudewijn, A. M. van Velzen, Coordinator International Projects
APS (National Centre for School Improvement),
Utrecht, The Netherlands

Preface

ISIP, the International School Improvement Project coordinated by the Organisation for Economic Cooperation and Development (OECD), began in 1982 and united fourteen OECD countries and their experts on the topic of school improvement. The project was formally ended in 1986 and resulted in a library of fourteen books and reports, summarising the knowledge of educational experts in the participating countries on school improvement. It is generally acknowledged that the ISIP body of knowledge on school improvement in the 1980s was an international foundation of the school improvement movement.

The professional network created in the 1980s remained intact by means of the Foundation for International Collaboration on School Improvement (FICSI). FICSI proved to be a network in which the members had irregular face-to-face contacts, but it did turn out to be a useful means of organising international conferences and workshops at the American Educational Research Association (AERA) annual meetings in the United States, and at the annual meetings of the International Congress for School Effectiveness and Improvement (ICSEI).

At AERA 92 in San Francisco, the board of FICSI decided it would be useful to make formal links with other networks, and the resulting connection with ICSEI made it possible to bring together for the first time two different ways of approaching the phenomenon of creating more effective schools, involving on the one hand the research knowledge on effectiveness and on the other hand the practical and research knowledge about school improvement. The resulting symposium at ICSEI '93 led to a conference in Cardiff in which the participants decided to lay out the outcomes of the meeting in a publication, in which basic ideas and concepts about school improvement would be linked to the knowledge we have about school effectiveness. Since then, numerous international experts in their different fields have been cooperating to generate the contents of this book. We estimate that we certainly have done more than update 'ISIP-knowledge' here, and we think that we have indeed coupled school improvement knowledge to the current body of knowledge about school effectiveness. By so doing we hope to have prepared a solid base for future activities and a further extension of our knowledge about how to make good schools.

The main authors of the book contributed to the discussions, wrote chapters and acted as final editors of the available drafts. In alphabetical order, they are:

- Robert Bollen, the Netherlands;
- Bert Creemers, the Netherlands;
- David Hopkins, the UK;
- Nijs Lagerweij, the Netherlands;
- David Reynolds, the UK;
- Louise Stoll, the UK.

The following persons contributed to the discussions, and contributed to chapters with their specific knowledge. In alphabetical order, they are:

- Gerard van den Hoven, the Netherlands;
- Boudewijn van Velzen, the Netherlands.

As participants in the discussions and as critical readers of the drafts we would like to acknowledge the help of the following:

- Karen S. Louis, the USA;
- Lieke Melchers, the Netherlands;
- Matthew B. Miles, the USA;
- Deborah Roody, the USA.

Finally, we would like to express our gratitude to the Algemeen Pedagogisch Studiecentrum (APS) in the Netherlands for supporting our efforts by offering facilities to enable us to meet and work together, and to the Foundation for International Collaboration on School Improvement for supporting our meetings over the last four years.

David Reynolds, Bert Creemers, Robert Bollen
Utrecht, 27 October 1995

Chapter 1

School effectiveness and school improvement
The intellectual and policy context

Robert Bollen

INTRODUCTION

Over the centuries there have been many approaches to the phenomenon 'school', and much has been said about it from many different points of view, including the philosophical, ideological, social, psychological, educational, political and so on. But it is only in the twentieth century that we have been systematically trying to build up a real body of knowledge about schools and what is happening in and around them. Basically, this body of knowledge is trying to give answers to two fundamental questions: what do schools really look like in their daily operations; and how do schools develop over time? The first approach is known as school effectiveness research, and is like taking a picture of a school and comparing that with pictures of other schools. The second approach is known as school improvement practice, and is like telling stories about development and change in schools. This volume will explore these two ways of looking at schools and will try to combine them, with the aim of producing practically based knowledge that is available immediately and that can be used to direct the development of schools towards a desired level of performance.

We should be aware of the fact that effectiveness research found its origins in the phenomenon of the ineffective school (Edmonds, 1979). If schools were really perfect, fulfilling their missions to the great satisfaction of pupils, parents, school boards and politicians at local and national level, nobody would ever have thought about 'more' or 'less' effectiveness, and if schools were a perfect work-environment for teachers, nobody would ever have wanted to start a process of school improvement with teachers through convincing them that improving their own performance is the right thing to do.

School effectiveness needs a definition, because the concept is not altogether clear. We cannot just look at the output of the black box called 'school'; we also have to measure the input into it. Because we have to deal with a very complex entity, we need indicators or factors that can be compared and, even when we have school effectiveness factors, it still is difficult to know whether we are looking at causes or effects. Because of this uncertainty, school effectiveness knowledge needs to be based on facts and figures derived from a substantial number of schools, which suggests the usually quantitative approach of school effectiveness. Having all this in mind, we might define school effectiveness as:

> the extent to which any (educational) organisation as a social system, given certain resources and means, fulfils its objectives without incapacitating its means and resources and without placing undue strain upon its members
>
> (Georgopoulos and Tannenbaum, 1957)

in which '(educational)' is an addition to what is in essence an organisational approach to effectiveness. The advantage of this definition is its possibility to relate the knowledge of school effectiveness with the knowledge of school improvement at the definitional level. The notion that the fulfilment of its objectives is related to certain given resources and means is a recognition of the fact that schools in different circumstances have different possibilities to accomplish certain levels of effectiveness. A definition like this also makes it clear that effectiveness can also be related to rather subjective judgements about 'undue strain upon its members', which is certainly an interesting contemporary item for teacher unions and professional associations!

Given this definition, we do not have to talk about the 'ineffective school', and could replace this notion by that of a 'school with a very low degree of effectiveness', but we could never talk of 'zero effectiveness', because in that case the school would be closed. And at the same time we know that all schools can be improved, because the level of effectiveness of all the elements that constitute a given school will never all be at the limit of their possibilities.

Within the explicit concept of 'effectiveness' according to the definition, we can understand the effort of school improvement as an attempt to overcome the problems and troubles caused by activities at schools with a low degree of effectiveness: those with too little 'output' given the amount of 'input'. If we look at the definition of school improvement used in the ISIP project of the OECD (van Velzen *et al.*, 1985), we find that it is:

> a systematic, sustained effort aimed at change in learning condi-
> tions and other related internal conditions in one or more schools,
> with the ultimate aim of accomplishing educational goals more
> effectively.

We can clearly see how school improvement relates to effectiveness, but we can also see that school improvement is aiming at the improvement of the learning process by mentioning explicitly 'learn- ing conditions and other related internal conditions'. At this defini- tional level there is much 'openness' about the nature of educational goals and, in fact, school improvement efforts have often aimed at a great variety of educational goals.

By bringing school effectiveness research and school improvement activities together, as is done in this volume, we can see school effectiveness research as an attempt to define effectiveness at the level of educational practice. In doing that, school effectiveness research is offering educational improvement 'means' and 'goals' to practi- tioners in school improvement. In turn, school improvement can deliver its concepts of the school, the learning environment and its understanding of the processes of change to practitioners in school effectiveness research, thus contributing to a greater usefulness of the research.

CONTEXTUAL CHANGES IN THE 1990s

The market principle

Pursued to its essence the market principle tells us that, if there is a need, the market will find a means to meet it, or if there is an interesting prospect, people will find the means (the money) to get it. The other side of the coin is that the fittest economically will survive best. It is also clear that market-driven economies do not care too much about the side-effects of their activities.

We should be aware, though, that the 'market principle' is but a rough approximation of processes that have been going on for centuries. Education has always been a solution for societal problems and has never been an institution for just the fortunate few. On the contrary, looking back we can see that education as a system was basically created by the fortunate few to solve the problems created by the poor or non-privileged groups of the population (Swaan, 1989). This has never been a perfectly designed process, but education can be perceived as the result of complex collective processes aiming at 'arrangements' to deal with tensions in the wider society. These arrangements as such are not stable, but have to be replaced by new arrangements in case of societal development. In times when the low morale and anti-social conduct of the 'have-nots' was a threat to the 'haves', education had the function of disciplining the pupils by means of religion and imposing strict rules of behaviour. In times when the nation state came to power, this power could only be exerted over a population that could read and write, and so education provided those basic skills. The Industrial Revolution began at a rather simple level, with very little need for skilled labour, but it induced a lot of related processes in which vocational and technical education was necessary, a process which increased during the automation period when unskilled labour was replaced by machinery. As a consequence, the educational system had to provide higher levels of skills and the learning period had to be lengthened.

Looking at contemporary times, we may be witnesses to the end of the arrangements in which full employment was a precondition for the welfare state. We are now living in an era in which unemployment rates are high and in which they do not function any more as a goal of economic success. Labour is now exported to underdeveloped countries, and at the same time we can see rapidly growing countries with economic systems that are threatening the traditional wealthy countries. Once more, educational systems have to provide solutions, this time for those traditionally wealthy countries to survive in a global market. But we are still in the beginning of that process and, so far, the educational system seems to be in an orientation phase.

In this phase we may expect to see a changing relationship between the educational institutions and their clients. Even use of these terms shows the changes going on, because at one time we would have talked about 'schools' and 'pupils', or 'students'. In a market-driven educational system, schools compete with each other with efforts to enlarge their catchment areas by pleasing their clients and ensuring their success in their educational careers. In such an educational system, educational authorities want as much value for money as they can get and they currently look for means to measure the effectiveness of the components of the educational system. The workers in the educational arena are now evaluated in terms of their results and 'work load', and are rewarded accordingly. The whole system as such may incline towards greater selectivity, though components of the system may try to survive by being non-selective.

There is one major problem in the increased use of market principles as the basic concept on which to organise education. It has been one of the basic human rights for every individual to be educated and, though in different countries this has been worked out in different ways, it is unthinkable for many that an educational system is excluding individuals or groups of individuals because they cannot buy what they need, or because society cannot provide work suitable for their capacities. So, however market driven the educational system may become, there will always be a need for a centrally defined and guaranteed minimum of educational facilities in the eyes of many.

We need to notice a couple of things more. If we were to go inside schools and enter the classrooms, we might not notice any influence of the market principle at all. The teaching/learning process has its own dynamics, and teachers and pupils, though often different in many ways, are the same in that they mostly set their goals in the short term. Within this perspective, it would be difficult to indicate exactly the impact of market principles separately from so many other influences. But if we take one step back and look at the ways curricula are delivered, learning situations are designed and testing is organised at individual teacher level, it is easier to see a tendency to deal with the interests of the society as well as of the pupils. Moving upwards within the system, we again meet market principles, with school leaders possessing entrepreneurial assignments and ambitions trying to increase their catchment areas and to spend their available resources in the best possible way. Moving upwards again, we see that debate outside the schools is increasingly based upon cost–benefit analysis.

Policy-making

Politics, certainly in democratic settings, reflects the values and trends in society, and that means that politicians dominantly participate in the processes that lead to new societal arrangements. If we focus on educational policies in relation to current societal developments, we can see that they have to solve several serious problems. In the first place there seems to be a discrepancy between the needs of society for a smaller number of highly educated and highly motivated workers in a world increasingly dominated by information flows of high intensity, speeding over the electronic highways, and the wants of an increasing number of the learners in the educational system to get a good share of societal prosperity at low personal cost, driven by over-ambitious expectations about their future and about the possibilities of security on the long term. The effectiveness of the educational system partly depends on the motivation of learners, which means that, with the decreasing motivation of large groups of society for learning, effectiveness is harder to attain.

In the second place, education is just one of the claims within each society upon national budgets. This means that, for political reasons, budget cuts for education might be inescapable. Politicians, and of course society, have to make choices about what is desirable and feasible in a world where unlimited expansion of the economic base has to be restricted to a level that our ecological base can still carry.

In the third place, the state is in the middle of a process of reconsidering its functions and its scope. Though education as a responsibility cannot be given up, the responsibility might be limited to the lower age levels of the system, or it could be mandated to other, non-state, parts of the system. If societal phenomena are determined by the interaction of people at the operational levels of institutions, then it makes sense to let them run their own organisations, because obviously the power is at that level. This also reduces of course political conflicts with higher levels of the infrastructure. It can also reduce national political concern about the budgetary problems of the system, delegating the problem to schools and teachers and having them responsible for the integration of future generations within society.

If future societal arrangements with regards to the educational system follow the trends as roughly described here, then the educational system of the twenty-first century, and the school of the twenty-first century, will not just look different but will also function differently. Within the educational system, the new arrangements imply a greater independence for the components of the system and, at the same time, an increase in managerial tasks and responsibilities. In practice, though, this decentralisation policy is often associated with a centralisation policy at higher levels of the system, for instance at the national level where evaluation and assessment is concentrated. But if schools are indeed having to take over many of the tasks that were once performed outside them, then the size of the institution becomes an important item. In many countries, educational institutions are getting bigger and bigger for many reasons, but mostly because of the economic advantages of sharing the facilities with more people and of providing the conditions for the teaching/learning process at lower cost. An important issue at the school level now becomes the budget and its limitations, which often generates difficult choices. The school leader increasingly has to be a book-keeper as well as a decision-maker.

This contextual pressure, initiated by financial policy motives at the national, regional or even local level, leads after a while to the need to develop managerial strategies that can cope with the size of the enlarged institutions, often generated by difficult and painful merger processes. It becomes clear that leadership in a big and complex educational organisation is somewhat different from the traditional 'charismatic' leadership that often induced high educational quality in the classroom or the small school. It soon becomes obvious that bureaucratic means may satisfy the organisational 'top' of the institution, but that this does not necessarily bring about desired effects.

Therefore, a second wave of decentralisation has arisen, now inside the enlarged institutes, trying to give birth to workable units in which bureaucratic procedures are brought down to a minimum and in which responsibility is given to those who are really doing the job: 'site based management' and 'teacher empowerment' are the descriptions of this process.

This independence of schools, and of sub-systems within schools, also has implications for the content of education and will lead to school-based curricula, and might even lead to different educational practices within one school. Though we must be aware of the fact that in traditional schools teachers often acted like little independent 'shopkeepers', 'selling' their knowledge in the way they liked best, we must also realise that the current development in the teaching profession is not aiming at the state of the autonomous teacher. Bringing back responsibility for the quality and effectiveness of education to teachers necessitates the notions of collegiality and teamwork. Again we could say that any development of a trend towards decentralisation implies a need for centralisation at the same time. If teachers are responsible for the implementation of the curriculum and for the effectiveness of the teaching/learning process, they will only be able to accomplish this responsibility within a framework of clear educational goals.

The focus of the teacher is on the group of pupils in the classroom and on their learning activities, and of course teachers make their pedagogic choices within the context of a curriculum. The curriculum, as the body of knowledge and skills which the teacher and his or her pupils will aim to acquire, has to be a given for at least two reasons. In the first place, though working in a small collegial sub-system, the teacher is still participating in a bigger 'whole' in which the pupils must find their way and must be enabled to do so. That implies the existence of something like a basic concept of the goal of the process that is accepted and worked at by all teachers who have to deal with the same group of pupils over the years. This basic concept should be built up with two major components: an agreement about the content of education in general, and an agreement about the nature of the teaching/learning process. The content can be decided at the national level in terms of a national curriculum, which does not exclude the possibility of school-specific additions to fine-tune the curriculum to local circumstances or to the specific culture of each school. Agreement about the nature of the teaching/learning process has to be accomplished much closer to the level of the classroom, and should be embedded in collegial professional relationships. This means, at the level of the individual school, a need for educational leadership and professional craftsmanship exceeding subject knowledge and classroom management. The new arrangements of educational organisation will certainly require the upgrading of the teachers' professionalism, or, to put it in a different perspective, the new arrangements will not work if the teachers reject their new responsibilities.

The second reason that the curriculum needs to be laid down is that, even in the new decentralised arrangements, schools are still societal institutions, spending public money to achieve public educational goals with their pupils or students. By formulating the curriculum at central level, it remains possible to take political responsibility for the quality of the educational system as a whole.

CULTURAL DIFFERENCES

The educational system is closely related to the culture of its environment, which means that there will always be differences between countries and also within countries. A school in the inner city and a school in a rural area will be different for many reasons, as will be a school in France and one in Norway. Nevertheless, the twenty-first century is likely to develop particular cultural features which, in the end, will influence educational processes and institutions all over the world.

Cultural development seems to be more complex than economic and political development, and often goes in somewhat contrary directions. This seems to be the case, for instance, at the very basic level of religion and general outlook on life. On the one hand there is a tendency towards individualisation in which norms, values and beliefs are based on some sort of eclecticism and agnosticism, and on the other hand we can see how group fundamentalism and mass conservatism takes hold of large groups in society. As a consequence, we see the development both of schools of a multi-cultural nature and schools based upon a very restrictive cultural conception.

The traditional cultural role of the school used to be to confirm and develop the features of the dominant culture of the national environment, or, if the school was situated in some underdeveloped area, to facilitate the integration of their clients into the dominant culture. Schools were part of the general societal arrangements to lower the tensions between separate segments of the society. Nowadays, the cultural pattern of society looks more complex than it used to be, and schools, and teachers as individuals, are unlikely to be guided by one clearly defined cultural concept, except in those schools based upon the pattern of cultural segregation. Moreover, we may assume that the position of the school as an institution in the changing nature of modern society is not all together clear. At the moment several options have been tried out and are available:

- the school is an instrument for selection of those who will be able to function in the higher social classes of the society, although it is clear that there is much more ambition among students than there are opportunities to satisfy them;
- the school is an instrument for a plural and multi-cultural population living peacefully together in society;
- the school is an instrument for personal development, in which differentiation of the teaching/learning process related to abilities and ambitions of individual pupils or students is the norm;
- the school is an instrument to guarantee every pupil or student a minimum level of attainment to function in the society as a worker at whatever level;
- combinations of these options within one educational system.

The trouble with these options is that the decision of which to choose cannot be made without a complicated political debate in which the conflicting interests of ideological, political and economic groups will clash, in times in which the old societal arrangements under pressure of increasing international cooperation, uncertain economic development and other significant demographic changes are not likely to present a basis for a consensus about choices and solutions.

It is within this context of hesitation and uncertainty that we need to take another look at the concept of the effective school. This concept can be perceived as an effort to define a school-specific organisational concept, fit to be used within the context of many other, wider, cultural concepts and in fact aiming at no more than an effective teaching/learning process. This vision is school-specific because the implementation of the concept is not really dependent upon factors outside the school and can be implemented within a wide variety of educational contexts. The advantage of this concept is that it is related to a core of school activities and can be translated into clearly visible behaviour, acceptable in almost any cultural environment.

This advantage is lost at the very moment that the concept of the effective school is no longer understood as being school-specific and is introduced as an organisation coupled to very strictly defined curricula. And if we want to take the linking of school improvement and school effectiveness seriously, it is important to see whether the emphasis on the teaching/learning process as the core business of the school and the aim of increasing the effectiveness of this process are basically any more than a technocratic approach to some problems that have been analysed in the functioning of the institution called 'school', or whether we are looking at a cultural concept in which the school reflects a holistic vision of society.

A cultural concept can be described as a conceptual map by which the participants in the school organisation can understand which attitudes and behaviours are preferred (Robbins, 1984). Taking a look at the essential features of the effective school (Mortimore *et al.*, 1988), we can easily recognise that most of them are of an attitudinal nature. Performing goal-oriented educational leadership means not just being well informed about goals and means in a given educational area and transferring this information adequately to the school team, but demands a whole array of personal qualities, effective strategies of monitoring and support, high quality leadership and, finally, the time to build up the trust to make that leadership effective. The implanting of an educational leader in a school which has no experience of such a vision of effectiveness will certainly cause something like a culture shock. Commitment of vice-principals and teachers to the cause of effectiveness is not just a personal matter for them, but a significant element contributing to school climate and culture. Even such a simple thing as the registration of pupils' progress is not just a technical operation, but will only work if teachers and pupils are part of a culture that will positively react to outcomes.

There is no doubt about it: the concept of the effective school is a cultural concept and is considerably more than a technique that can be learned by the school team in a series of training sessions.

In terms of encouraging school improvement towards greater effectiveness, this is an important and maybe even surprising statement. It means that the effective school never can be implemented by some sort of organisationally based, top-down improvement strategy. Of course, we can think of conditions that will promote the development of greater effectiveness, like enhanced public accountability of schools, a fiscal regime that will reward effectiveness and penalise ineffectiveness, and a public debate to persuade actors and stakeholders of the intrinsic values of the concept of effectiveness. But the measurement of effectiveness will be a precarious business, because the indicators for effectiveness will by their nature be indicators of a limited definition of effectiveness and may simply invite schools to use strategies to cheat.

Improvement towards effectiveness will have to lean upon teachers' willingness to adopt a different cultural, as well as organisational, view on their own profession. It is clear that school effectiveness is mainly determined by classroom effectiveness, which brings the teaching/learning process into the centre of the improvement process. The teacher's role is a very important variable in the determination of effectiveness. But the other side of the coin is that teachers' roles should change. This change is simple to describe, but difficult to attain, but we realise that we are aiming at a change in the learning conditions by changing the role of the teacher.

To make the effective school work, we need improvement strategies that will mould teachers' cultures and behaviours in such a way that pupil behaviour will change. The effective school is, in the end, characterised by the effective behaviour of its learners. The teachers can be held responsible for that, and the school has to create and sustain the climate and the culture in which an effective teaching/learning process will flourish.

THE CONCEPTUALISATION OF THE SCHOOL

A school is a very complex entity in itself, and is part of a complex educational system with local and national components. There are many ways of looking at schools and school systems. Even in this volume, in which we try to bring school effectiveness research and school improvement strategies together, we can see several concepts used to explain why and how schools need to be improved towards more effectiveness.

A very basic conceptualisation of the school is to look at the school as an input–throughput–output system. This concept has been useful for effectiveness research, because a reduction to this simple idea is easily realised. In this model, there is no need to look at the 'throughput' phase, which would bring about an enormous increase in the number of relevant factors. It is mainly the 'throughput' portion of the concept that is very difficult to analyse because of its complexity and because a lot of the key elements within this phase are difficult to observe. It is almost impossible to measure key factors like the motivation, the willingness, the capability and the capacity to improve of *all* the important actors within the system. It is obvious that school improvement knowledge needs considerably more insight in the throughput phase than the model as such can deliver. On the other hand, it is a very useful model to assess results, taking into consideration the fact that improvement which does not affect the results of the school will not be tolerated by the environment outside the school.

The outside-school environment, as well as the content of the 'black box' of the school itself, gets a lot of attention in another model. Here, the school and the environment are brought together in a centralisation in which the school and the educational system are perceived as consisting of multiple levels upon which many different educational actors play their role in determining the effectiveness of the system and of single schools.

Indeed, an important contribution of the school improvement approach has been the recognition of the importance of the existence of different levels in the educational system. Even if we look at just one school, we can recognise several levels of actors with different tasks, responsibilities and influence. But even if we consider the school as the unit of change, we will have to take account of the outside-school environment, which is also structured in levels.

School effectiveness research recognises the importance of the concept of the level, but from a different point of view. In the search for factors that contribute to school effectiveness, it is clear that those factors are not just concerned with the interaction between teacher and pupil, because knowledge about the characteristics of effective schools has increased tremendously in the period since Edmonds formulated his five factors to distinguish effective schools from ineffective schools (Edmonds, 1979). In Chapter Three of this volume, for example, a comprehensive model for further research is developed in which all the relevant factors from the multiple levels, which have influence on the effectiveness of the teaching/learning process, are combined (Creemers, 1994). These factors can be perceived as subjects for further research, in order to increase our understanding of what really contributes to the effectiveness of schools.

In most cases of school improvement, different levels have to cooperate and be dependent upon each other, and this interaction between the levels and the cooperation of the levels happens to be an important aspect of any successful improvement effort. Strategies have to be based on an understanding of the internal dynamics of the educational system, which can mostly be explained by the characteristics of the actors at the different levels. Basic questions are:

- Who, on what level, is initiating the improvement?
- Who on what level, is involved?
- Who is aiming at what objective(s)?

Using the notion of levels, we can show the way in which school effectiveness and school improvement are linked. We should not overestimate the value of such a model, but it enables us to see where conceptual links can be established between the two bodies of knowledge, though without necessarily showing how the links can be worked out in practice.

This introduces another concept of the school that is useful in bringing together school improvement and school effectiveness: the concept of the school as a learning organisation (Senge, 1990). It is obvious that school improvement is only possible if the school as an organisation is capable of learning, not just in the case of individuals like teachers or school leaders but in such a way that the school itself is able to overcome ineffective behaviour by close cooperation. Given the relatively autonomous position of teachers, the school as a learning organisation will only initially really develop by means of educational leadership, wherever this is located in the organisation. It is interesting that effectiveness research mentions 'strong educational leadership' as an important factor in school effectiveness, while, in the more school improvement oriented concept of the school as a learning organisation, educational leadership is also emphasised. The educational leader of the school seems to be a key person in the integration of school effectiveness and school improvement, and in making the notion of school improvement towards more effectiveness really work.

THE CONCEPT OF IMPROVEMENT

To be able to think about school improvement we need not just a concept of the school as an object of improvement but also a clear concept of what we mean when we talk about improvement, and in particular about school improvement.

In Chapter Four we have an overview of how our understanding of school improvement has developed over the last thirty years. At this point we only want to give some initial notions about school improvement as they were developed in the original OECD funded ISIP project, mentioned in the Preface to this volume (van Velzen *et al.*, 1985).

An important notion related to this notion of improvement is that improvement takes time, or, in other words, school improvement is a process, not an event. This is the basic concept behind school improvement, which has a strong influence on many other concepts of school improvement. A similar important notion is that school improvement is not linear, and cannot be easily understood within a technological, rational paradigm (Van Velzen *et al.*, 1985).

Nevertheless, it is important to distinguish within this undoubtedly non-linear process the different phases of the process. The scheme in Figure 1.1 is strongly related to the school improvement notion in which diagnosis plays an important role, the so-called 'school-based review' strategy (Bollen and Hopkins, 1987). This is really a simple part of the improvement process, but is not to be seen as a purely linear model. It identifies several phases in which an improvement process, or rather elements of an improvement process, can begin. It also makes clear whether a given improvement process has really gone through all the important phases, and it also helps to focus on the specific phases of the process.

In practice, almost any improvement effort can be divided into sub-processes which are not necessarily proceeding simultaneously in the same phase.

Phases of the process of improvement
0 Preparation
1 Diagnostic phase
2 Strategic planning phase
3 Developmental phase
4 Evaluation phase

Figure 1.1 The process of improvement

For our purpose, this schema can help us to make better links between school effectiveness and school improvement. It is obvious that any diagnosis implicates judgements. In schools, a lot of diagnosis does not exceed the level of an opinion and in a lot of improvement projects objectives for improvement are chosen or adopted without taking a thorough look at the current state of affairs, and in many cases without very much knowledge about the educational required standards. It is here that school effectiveness knowledge can help. By looking at the factors that contribute to school effectiveness which can be handled by the actors at a given level, it is possible to identify objectives for improvement that will really help to improve effectiveness. With a focus on those factors, diagnosis will provide a strong base for further actions. Use of school effectiveness knowledge will give the diagnosis phase of the improvement process more meaning. At the same time, school effectiveness knowledge will increase when the improvement effort shows how much difference it makes to achieving the chosen objectives.

Looking at the strategic planning phase again, school effectiveness knowledge will help strategic planners to keep in mind that, ultimately, the effectiveness of the school has to be delivered at the classroom level, and in particular in the actual teaching/learning process. School effectiveness knowledge illuminates what is this core activity in schools and what is conditional for it to improve. Planning for effectiveness will be inadequate without that focus.

In the phase of development, school improvers need more knowledge about what causes what in terms of effectiveness, and it seems that at this phase effectiveness knowledge has less to offer than is needed.

Looking at the last phase of the scheme, it is important that evaluation should be included in any process aiming at improvement.

School improvers will often perform evaluation activities in the shape of a case study, or, at a lower level of the system, just orally, in some sort of evaluative meeting. However, school improvers, certainly if we are dealing with reforms of some scale, should evaluate their projects in such a way that they can contribute to the validity of school effectiveness knowledge.

It is obvious that thinking about school improvement as a process can only be useful by relating this concept of 'phases' to the concept of the levels in the system and the schools, as was noted above. In this volume we will see that it is illuminating to integrate both schemes into one. This is also important because it is a key concept of school improvement that improvement processes are the result of the synchronicity of internal needs and external pressure.

SOME PROBLEMS WITH EFFECTIVENESS RESEARCH

Effectiveness research, as well as school improvement practice, does have specific characteristics which generate specific problems with respect to making contributions to a common base of knowledge. Looking at the characteristics of school effectiveness research, it is obvious just by the fact that we are looking at research that the basis and the use of the knowledge is situated in universities or comparable institutes. Even in this volume there is a difference between the chapters devoted to effectiveness research and those devoted to school improvement, in terms of their practicality. The knowledge offered by effectiveness research needs a lot of modification and translation before it will be applicable at the school level.

It is important to note that the ultimate goal of research is to gather knowledge, and not necessarily to generate a programme for improvement. Such a programme can of course be based upon the knowledge produced by effectiveness research, as is well demonstrated in this volume, but doing this will never be the basic aim of the research as a discipline. This state of affairs has much to do with the methodological base of school effectiveness research and, in particular, with its use of quantitative data. The research shows the complexity of the school in its societal function, with specific organisational features dealing with the teaching/learning process as its main task. It is difficult for practitioners to recognise their own environment if it is disaggregated into small 'factors'.

This need for scientific evidence is another barrier which prevents school effectiveness research from delivering clear messages at the school door. Within the methodological framework of effectiveness research, it is difficult to get real evidence of what causes what in schools and school systems, as is clearly outlined in Chapter Five. This is even more the case in international comparative research, because cultural and political differences between countries add tremendously to the complexity of the research designs. In Chapter Three we see that characteristics which play an important role in the determination of positive outcomes in one country only produce a weak correlation in other countries.

Finally, we may apply our concept of the levels in the educational system to the problem we are dealing with: the transfer of effectiveness research knowledge to practitioners in improving schools, or to groups of actors within school teams. Levels in the system are often considered almost as closed systems, and there is often a language problem between the levels. Messages from one level to another are seldom understood by the receivers with the same meaning which had been intended by the senders. In fact, the same phenomenon is obvious if we look at the transfer of knowledge from the research level to the political level. In both cases, the messages are deciphered within the frameworks of existing interests and prevailing judgements inherent to the level on which the receivers are performing.

PROBLEMS WITH SCHOOL IMPROVEMENT

Thinking in terms of furthering cooperation between effectiveness research on the one hand and school improvement practice on the other, we should not put all the blame on effectiveness research in explaining why there has been difficulty in taking useful things from each other. In school improvement, as well, we can see some problems inherent in the nature of its knowledge base which make it difficult to integrate this specific body of knowledge with effectiveness knowledge.

School improvement generates its knowledge differently from effectiveness research. While effectiveness research deals with characterics of a measurable nature which are mostly correlates in statistical overviews, school improvement focuses on processes and tries to describe them in case stories. It is clear that a case study is still a story and that a knowledge base founded on case stories might not be reliable in all aspects. We can see that school improvement is often attempting to upgrade the case study knowledge base by relating it back to models in which the dynamics of processes are made understandable by summaries. This contributes to the understanding of the improvement processes, but at the same time it needs a lot of translation and explanation. We even see that sometimes the core of school improvement knowledge is summarised and brought back to a metaphor, such as that 'change is a journey, not a blueprint' (Fullan, 1993).

School improvement knowledge, in contrast to effectiveness research knowledge, in its base and in its utilisation is *practical* knowledge, not really tied to strong methodological standards. The ultimate goal of school improvement knowledge has been to provide the change facilitator with skills for, and an understanding of, school improvement (Bollen, 1993). This means that school improvement knowledge has always to be transferred into improvement strategies, built on a series of interventions by different actors in the improving system.

While effectiveness research is trying to get an answer to the question, 'is the evidence for this specific correlation between a school characteristic and results valid?', school improvement is particularly interested in the question, 'does this improvement strategy work, and is this intervention in these circumstances effective?' It is easy to understand that the differences in disciplines and their approaches to the same object are major obstacles for a fruitful dialogue between school effectiveness researchers and school improvement practitioners. Nevertheless, later on we attempt to give a strong stimulus to the improvement of this dialogue, which is the essence of this volume.

WHY EFFECTIVENESS RESEARCH AND SCHOOL IMPROVEMENT PRACTICE SHOULD BE LINKED

The challenge for the coming years is to integrate the two bodies of knowledge, and this volume attempts to make a contribution to this process. With the schemes described in this chapter in mind, we will try to arrange the available knowledge in such a way that both bodies of knowledge can be coupled together in one scheme and one frame of reference.

In Chapter Two we will explore the goals of education as seen in school effectiveness research, in order to set objectives for improvement. In Chapter Three we will then outline the nature of the existing knowledge within school effectiveness. After that it will be time to look at what we know about school improvement, and this is done in

Chapter Four. There is a firm body of knowledge, but we also have to admit that some of the findings are still very context bound ar d some areas need further exploration. We will try to focus in particular on 'useful' knowledge, by which we mean knowledge that can be used in future improvement work with the ultimate aim of making schools more effective.

After conducting this overview of both school effectiveness knowledge and school improvement knowledge, we will try to 'make better links' between the two in Chapter Five, which indicates that we will take notice of the differences and the commonalities between them. The differences have to do with the differences between researchers and practitioners on the one hand, but also with the methodology and the conceptual base on the other. Those differences cannot be denied, but we will try to develop a common frame of reference.

Finally, we will come in Chapter Six to outlining the newly emerging practice of 'school improvement towards effectiveness', in which use of the two bodies of knowledge is evident. Expressed diagrammatically, the structure of the book is shown in Figure 1.2.

Chapter 2:
The effectiveness and quality of education
The criteria for objectives for the improvement process

Chapter 3:	Chapter 5:	Chapter 4:
The body of knowledge of school effectiveness	The process of going back and forth between the two bodies of knowledge within an integrated scheme	The body of knowledge of school improvement with an emphasis on strategies, processes and actors

Chapter 6:
Recent and cutting edge practice in merging school effectiveness/improvement

Figure 1.2 The structure of this book

REFERENCES

Bollen, R. and Hopkins, D. (1987) *School Based Review: towards a praxis*, Leuven: ACCO.

Bollen, R. (ed.) (1993) *Educational Change Facilitators: craftsmanship and effectiveness*, Utrecht: National Centre for School Improvement.

Creemers, B. P. M. (1994) *The quality of education* (De kwaliteit van het onderwijs). Report of a conference of the Groningen Institute for Educational Research (GION).

Edmonds, R. R. (1979) 'Effective schools for the urban poor', *Educational Leadership* 37(1).

Fullan, M. (1993) *Change Forces, Probing the Depths of Educational Reform*, London: Falmer Press, 37–42.

Georgopoulos, B. S. and Tannenbaum, A. S. (1957) 'A study of organizational effectiveness', *American Sociological Review*, 22(5), 534–40.

Mortimore, P., Sammons, P., Stoll, L., Lewis, D. and Ecob, R. (1988) *School Matters*, Berkeley: University of California Press.

Robbins, S. P. (1984) *Essentials of Organizational Behaviour*, London: Prentice-Hall.

Senge, P. (1990) *The Fifth Discipline*, New York: Random House.

Swaan, A. de (1989) *In Care of the State: Health care, education and welfare in Europe and the USA in the Modern Era*, London/New York: Routledge & Kegan Paul.

Velzen, W. G. van, Miles, M. B., Ekholm, M., Hameyer, U. and Robin, D. (1985) *Making School Improvement Work*, Leuven: ACCO.

Chapter 2

The goals of school effective and school improvement

Bert Creemers

INTRODUCTION

On pp. 18–19 we outlined what we are undertaking as the intellectual and practical aim of this book – the generation of knowledge in the rapidly changing educational world of the 1990s that will be as useful as was the knowledge formerly generated by the International School Effectiveness Research Project in the 1980s. We also outlined how we will look widely into numerous areas and paradigms – school effectiveness, school improvement, educational evaluation – in our search for the 'really useful knowledge' that we need to address our themes.

This chapter begins our task by looking at the ways in which different educational groups have conceptualised and measured the goals of education. Indeed, all researchers in the field of educational effectiveness and all practitioners involved in school improvement face the problem of deciding on their criteria for educational effectiveness and educational improvement. Any discussion about the effectiveness and improvement of education implies an idea about what is 'effective' and what is 'improvement'. In such discussions quite often not only the terms 'effectiveness' or 'improvement' are used, but participants talk about the 'quality' of education of a class or of a school. The term 'quality' is rather vague because it can include almost anything, such as effectiveness, efficiency, and statements about the content, processes, and inputs of education. That is the reason why we prefer the term 'effectiveness' (Creemers, 1994), which refers to means–ends relationships between educational processes and student outcomes.

When we use the term 'quality' later in the text we use it in a restricted sense, and we refer to the effectiveness of education and to research on the causes of effectiveness. Improvement refers to educational change that enhances student outcomes and, in this way, concerns changes towards more effectiveness (van Velzen *et al.*, 1985; Hopkins *et al.*, 1994). So, effectiveness and improvement are clearly related to each other conceptually.

Related to the criteria for effectiveness is the problem of what induces effectiveness and improvement. Because researchers and practitioners are involved in what constitutes and what leads to school effectiveness and school improvement, there is a good chance that they will exchange goals and means (Fullan, 1991). For example, they talk about 'educational leadership' as a goal in itself, instead of as a means to achieve more effective education, while ultimately changes in educational leadership are contributions to the improvement towards more effective education (Bamburg and Andrews, 1991; Leithwood, 1992). Later in the text we will have to determine what we label as 'effective school' or 'effective classroom education'.

Researchers are interested in the development and the testing of a theory about what induces effectiveness: about which factors, which characteristics of education lead to effectiveness, or to put it another way, what causes the differences in effectiveness between schools (Scheerens, 1993). The same holds for practitioners involved in school improvement. They are involved in how to generate effectiveness in schools; in other words, they generate the differences in change processes to achieve the higher effectiveness of schools (Stoll and Fink, 1994). Most parties are looking for the components of education, for the behaviour of principals and teachers, for example, that can differ between classrooms, schools, and educational systems. This may lead to the conclusion that, when we see more of a certain kind of behaviour or more of a certain factor in classrooms, in schools and in the educational system, then that classroom, school, or system has a higher quality. In several research traditions, factors such as leadership, educational climate and the structure of teaching are measured, and from these measurements inferences are made about the effectiveness of a school. However, factors such as structuring and climate and so on are not about high effectiveness *in themselves*, but their importance is based on the fact that they *lead to* effectiveness.

The criteria for educational effectiveness have to be defined in another way. They should be something other than the characteristics and features of education in classrooms, in schools and in the educational system. These criteria for effectiveness and improvement

- the availability of an indicator system and/or a national policy on evaluation/a national testing system;
- training and support which promotes effective schools and instruction;
- the funding of schools based on outcomes.

Time refers to:

- national guidelines with respect to the time schedules of schools;
- supervision of the maintenance of schedules.

Opportunity to learn refers to:

- national guidelines and rules with respect to the development of the curriculum, the school working plan and the activity plan at the school level, for example through a national curriculum.

It is clear that, at the different levels, and especially at the context level, resources are also important, but resources should be operationalised as such things as the availability of materials, teachers and other components supporting education in schools and classrooms (Hanushek, 1989; Gray, 1990; Hedges *et al.*, 1994), rather than as a more general, global level of financial resources.

At the context level, consistency, constancy and control are again important formal characteristics which can be utilised, emphasising the importance of the same characteristics over time and of mechanisms to ensure synchronicity at a point in time.

CONCLUSIONS

It can be seen that school effectiveness research has revealed a considerable number of characteristics of effective schools. These factors can be found at the level of the classroom (especially in the case of instructional factors), the level of the school (especially in the case of organisational and curriculum arrangements) and at the context level (which encompasses the community, the district, and the state). It is probable that factors at all these levels can contribute to learning outcomes, broadly defined as learning results.

It is also clear that we have made considerable progress over the years, both in elucidating these effective school characteristics and in understanding *how* they have their apparent effects. The recent development of models of effectiveness that are both multi-level and attempt to look at the relationships and the synchronicity between levels is seen as particularly useful in generating a 'technology' of practice that can provide a foundation of knowledge for those who wish to modify and improve schools.

REFERENCES

Bloom, B. S. (1976) *Human Characteristics and School Learning*, New York: McGraw-Hill.

Brookover, W. B., Beady, C., Flood, P. and Schweitzer, J. (1979) *School Systems and Student Achievement: Schools Make a Difference*, New York: Praeger.

Brophy, J. and Good, T. L. (1986) 'Teacher behavior and student achievement', in M. C. Wittrock (ed.), *Handbook of Research on Teaching* (pp. 328–75), New York: Macmillan.

Carroll, J. B. (1963) 'A model of school learning', *Teachers College Record*, 64(8), 723–33.

Coleman, J. S., Campbell, E. Q., Hobson, C. F., McPartland, J., Mood, A. M., Weinfeld, F. D. and York, R. L. (1966) *Equality of Educational Opportunity*, Washington, DC: US Government Printing Office.

Creemers, B. P. M. (1983) 'De bijdrage van onderwijsonderzoek aan de verhoging van de kwaliteit van het onderwijs' (The contribution of educational research to the enhancement of the quality of education), in B. P. M. Creemers, W. Hoeben and K. Koops (eds), *De Kwaliteit van het onderwijs* (The quality of education), (pp. 215–32), Haren/Groningen: RION/Wolters–Noordhoff.

—— (1991) *Effectieve instructie: een empirische bijdrage aan de verbetering van het onderwijs in de klas* (Effective instruction: an empirical contribution to improvement of education in the classroom), 's-Gravenhage: SVO.

—— (1994) *The Effective Classroom*, London: Cassell.

Creemers, B. P. M. and Osinga, N. (1995) *ICSEI Country Reports*, Leeuwarden: GCO.

Creemers, B. P. M. and Schaveling, J. (1985) *Verhoging van onderwijseffectiviteit* (Improving educational effectiveness), Den Haag: WRR.

Doyle, W. (1986) 'Classroom organization and management', in M. C. Wittrock (ed.), *Handbook of Research on Teaching*, (pp. 392–431), New York: Macmillan.

Edmonds, R. R. (1979) 'Effective schools for the urban poor', *Educational Leadership*, 37(1), 15–27.

Emmer, E. T. (1987) 'Classroom management', in M. J. Dunkin (ed.), *The International Encyclopedia of Teaching and Teacher Education*, (pp. 437–46), Oxford: Pergamon Press.

Evertson, C. M. and Green, J. L. (1986) 'Observation as inquiry and method', in M. C. Wittrock (ed.), *Handbook of Research on Teaching*, New York: Macmillan.

Flanders, N. (1970) *Analyzing Teacher Behavior*, Reading, MA: Addison-Wesley.

Fraser, B. J. (1986) *Classroom Environment*, London: Croom Helm.

Fullan, M. (1991) *The New Meaning of Educational Change*, London: Cassell.
Gage, N. L. (ed.) (1963) *Handbook of Research on Teaching*, Chicago: Rand McNally.
—— (1966) 'Research on cognitive aspects on teaching', in Association for Supervision and Curriculum Development, Seminar on Teaching, *The Way Teaching Is*, Washington, DC: National Education Association.
—— (1972) *Teacher Effectiveness and Teacher Education. The search for a scientific basis*, Palo Alto, CA: Pacific Books.
Gray, J. (1990) 'The quality of schooling: frameworks for judgements', *British Journal of Educational Studies*, 38(3), 204–33.
Gray, J., Jesson, D., Goldstein, H., Hedger, K. and Rasbash, J. (1995) 'A multi-level analysis of school improvement: Changes in schools' performance over time', *School Effectiveness and School Improvement*, 6(2), 97–115.
Grift, W. van de (1990) 'Educational leadership and academic achievement in elementary education', *School Effectiveness and School Improvement*, 1(1), 26–40.
Hanushek, E. A. (1989) 'The impact of differential expenditures on school performance', *Educational Researcher*, 18(4), 45–65.
Hedges, L. V., Laine, R. D. and Greenwald, R. (1994) 'Does money matter? A meta-analysis of studies of the effects of differential school inputs on student outcomes', *Educational Researcher*, 23(3), 5–14.
Hopkins, D., Ainscow, M. and West, M. (1994) *School Improvement in an Era of Change*, London: Cassell.
International School Effectiveness Research Programme (ISERP) (1992) *An Outline*, Cardiff: University of Wales.
Levine, D. U. and Lezotte, L. W. (1990) *Unusually effective schools: a review and analysis of research and practice*, Madison: National Center for Effective Schools Research and Development.
Luyten, H. (1994) *School Effects: Stability and malleability*, Enschede: University of Twente.
Mortimore, P., Sammons, P., Stoll, L., Lewis, D. and Ecob, R. (1988) *School Matters: The Junior Years*, Wells: Open Books.
Ralph, J. H. and Fennessey, J. (1983) 'Science or reform: some questions about the effective schools model', *Phi Delta Kappan*, 64(10), 689–94.
Reezigt, G. J. and Creemers, B. P. M. (1995) 'Conditions for the effectiveness of instruction at the school level', *School Effectiveness and School Improvement* (submitted).
Reynolds, D. (1976) 'The delinquent school', in P. Woods (ed.), *The Process of Schooling*, London: Routledge and Kegan Paul.
—— (1982) 'The search for effective schools', *School Organisation*, 2(3), 215–37.
Reynolds, D., Creemers, B. P. M., Nesselrodt, P. S., Schaffer, E. C., Stringfield, S. and Teddlie, C. (eds) (1994) *Advances in School Effectiveness Research and Practice*, Oxford: Pergamon Press.
Reynolds, D., Sammons, P., Stoll, L., Barber, M. and Hillman, J. (1996) 'School Effectiveness and School Improvement in the United Kingdom', in *School Effectiveness and School Improvement* (in press).
Rosenholtz, S. J. (1989) *Teachers' Workplace*, New York: Longman.

Rosenshine, B. (1979) 'Content, time and direct instruction', in P. L. Peterson and H. J. Walberg (eds), *Research on Teaching*, Berkeley, CA: McCutchan.
Rutter, M., Maughan, B., Mortimore, P. and Ouston, J. (1979) *Fifteen Thousand Hours*, London: Open Books.
Scheerens, J. (1992) *Effective Schooling: Research, theory and practice*, London: Cassell.
Scheerens, J. and Creemers, B. P. M. (1989) 'Conceptualizing school effectiveness', *International Journal of Educational Research*, 13(7), 691–706.
Scheerens, J., Vermeulen, C. J. A. J. and Pelgrum, W. J. (1989) 'Generalizibility of instructional and school effectiveness indicators across nations', *International Journal of Educational Research*, 13 (7), 789–99.
Stringfield, S. (1994) 'A model of elementary school effects', in D. Reynolds, B. P. M. Creemers, P. S. Nesselrodt, E. C. Schaffer, S. Stringfield and C. Teddlie (eds), *Advances in School Effectiveness Research and Practice*, (pp. 153–87), Oxford: Pergamon Press.
—— (1995) 'Attempting to enhance students' learning through innovative programs: The case for schools evolving into High Reliability Organizations', *School Effectiveness and School Improvement*, 6(1), 67–96.
Stringfield, S. C. and Slavin, R. E. (1992) 'A hierarchical longitudinal model for elementary school effects', in B. P. M. Creemers and G. J. Reezigt (eds), *Evaluation of Educational Effectiveness*, (pp. 35–69), Groningen: ICO.
Stringfield, S., Teddlie, C., Wimpleberg, R. K. and Kirby, P. (1992) 'A five year follow-up of schools in the Louisiana School Effectiveness Study', in J. Bashi and Z. Sass (eds), *School Effectiveness and School Improvement: Proceedings of the Third International Congress, Jerusalem*, Jerusalem: The Magness Press.
Teddlie, C. and Stringfield, S. (1993) *Schools Make a Difference: Lessons Learned from a 10-year Study of School Effects*, New York: Teachers College Press.
Travers, R. M. W. (ed.) (1973) *Second Handbook of Research on Teaching*, Chicago: Rand McNally.
Veenman, S., Lem, P., Roelofs, E. and Nijssen, F. (1992) *Effectieve instructie en doelmatig klassemanagement* (Effective instruction and adequate classroom management), Amsterdam: Swets and Zeitlinger.
Vermeulen, C. J. (1987) 'De effectiviteit van onderwijs bij zeventien Rotterdamse stimuleringsscholen' (Educational effectiveness in seventeen educational priority schools in Rotterdam), *Pedagogische Studiën*, 64, 49–58.
Weide, M. G. (1995) *Effectief basisonderwijs voor allochtone leerlingen* (Effective elementary education for ethnic minority students), Groningen: RION.
Werf, M. P. C. van der (1995) *The Educational Priority Policy in the Netherlands: Content, Implementation and Outcomes*, Den Haag: SVO.
Wittrock, M. C. (ed.) (1986) *Handbook of Research on Teaching* (3rd ed.), New York: Macmillan.

Chapter 4

The school improvement knowledge base

David Hopkins and Nijs Lagerweij

INTRODUCTION

We have seen in Chapter 3 that a considerable body of knowledge has accumulated on the characteristics of schools that are effective in 'adding value' to their students. We now proceed to examine the core beliefs, the bodies of knowledge and the practical enterprises produced by researchers and practitioners in the field of school improvement. An attempt is made to organise the field by looking in turn at:

- the history of the study of change and school improvement;
- the centralisation–decentralisation paradox;
- definitions of school improvement and school development;
- the process of school improvement;
- a framework for school improvement efforts;
- some of the most common school improvement strategies;
- six propositions for successful school improvement efforts;
- the theoretical implications for school improvement.

THE STUDY OF SCHOOL CHANGE AND SCHOOL IMPROVEMENT

The development of knowledge in the area of educational change has a capricious nature and shows much resemblance to the process of trial and error, in which insight grows, as experience with attempts at educational change grows. Over a period of thirty years of research on change in schools, it seems that people with very different sets of beliefs have tried to implement change in education. In general, and as Fullan (1991) has previously noted, one can state that in every decade there is a new perspective on the way such processes should be managed (for a review of thirty years of educational change in the United States, see Sashkin and Egermeier, 1992).

The first, which dates from the mid-1960s, was the emphasis on the *adoption of curriculum materials*. On both sides of the Atlantic, the curriculum reform movement was intended to have a major impact on student achievement through the production and dissemination of exemplary curriculum materials. Although the materials were often of high quality, being produced by teams of academics and psychologists, in the main they failed to have an impact on teaching. The reason is obvious in hindsight; teachers were not included in the production process and the in-service training that accompanied the new curricula was often perfunctory and rudimentary. Teachers simply took what they thought was of use from the new materials and integrated them into their own teaching. The curriculum innovation, however, was consequently subverted.

The second phase – covering most of the 1970s – was essentially one of *documenting failure*, the failure of the curriculum reform movement to affect practice. It became increasingly apparent from this work that 'top-down' models of change did not work, that teachers required in-service training to acquire new knowledge and skills, and that implementation did not occur spontaneously as a result of legislative fiat. It was clear that implementation is an extremely complex and lengthy process that requires a sensitive combination of strategic planning and individual learning and commitment to succeed. Much was learned about implementation during this period that was to lay the basis for future work.

The third phase, roughly from the late 1970s to the mid-1980s, was a *period of success*. It was during this time that the first studies of school effectiveness were published (Rutter *et al.*, 1979; Reynolds, 1985), and that a consensus was established as to the characteristics of effective schools (Purkey and Smith, 1983; Wilson and Corcoran, 1988). This is not meant to imply, however, that this line of enquiry has been unproblematic; there is still much more work to be done, as Chapter Three illustrates. It was also during this period that some major large-scale studies of school improvement projects were conducted (Crandall *et al.*, 1982, 1986; Hargreaves *et al.*, 1984; Huberman and Miles, 1984; Rosenholtz, 1989; Louis and Miles, 1990). Much was consequently learned about the dynamics of the change process. As can be seen later, the OECD International School Improvement Study (ISIP) was also at work at this time, producing case studies of and developing strategies for school improvement (for an overview, see van Velzen *et al.*, 1985; Hopkins, 1987). A number of syntheses of the work during this period also appeared, of which the contributions of Fullan (1985) and Joyce and his colleagues (1983) are very important.

Although this creative period produced knowledge of increasing specificity about the change process and the factors influencing effective schooling, this was a necessary but not sufficient condition to improve the quality of education. As Fullan (1991) points out, clear descriptions of success are not tantamount to solving the problem of the management of change towards that success.

Managing Change, the fourth phase, which has been recently entered, will prove to be the most difficult and hopefully the most productive of all, as researchers and practitioners struggle to relate their strategies and their research knowledge to the realities of schools in a pragmatic, systematic and sensitive way. There is indeed now a move away from studying change as a phenomenon to actually participating in school development, and the best of the current work on educational change is coming from people who are actually studying change as they are engaged in bringing it about. Research knowledge and 'change theory' is being refined through action (Fullan, 1993). Recent school improvement projects, described in Chapter Six, provide the application of school improvement knowledge to the 'real world' of schools in an attempt to develop practical strategies for empowerment.

House (1981) has described three perspectives that have been dominant in studies on innovation. These perspectives are the technological, the political and the cultural perspectives (for a similar distinction, see also Tichy, 1983). A perspective, as used here, is a broad heuristic device containing presuppositions, values and perceptions of fact within a professional consensus of what is desirable, feasible and important. Research studies and policies have been conducted from one or more of these perspectives. Each perspective focuses upon different aspects of reality and values the same aspects differently. The technological perspective embodies a production image. Teaching is seen as a technique that can be analysed by subdividing it into its components, and improved by systematically developing better teaching forms and diffusing them to schools, which adopt them and put them into practice. The political perspective acknowledges the legitimate differences of interests in groups involved. Conflict, bargaining and the application of power are all recognised to exert influences on school change efforts. The cultural perspective values the basic notion of the importance of shared beliefs and values within groups, and suggests that innovations require the interaction of separate cultures.

While researchers and policy-makers have seemed to lend themselves to one or other of these perspectives, it is important to realise that the three perspectives are related to one another. Each perspective focuses on different aspects of reality, and, in fact, values the same differently. It will be obvious as we move through this chapter that it seems sensible to use *all* perspectives in developing and implementing innovations in education.

The importance of the management of change is also connected with the new educational policies in different countries. These educational policies aim at the creation of the more autonomous school, which has a degree of space for the generation of policy to determine in some cases goals and in some cases educational means. These policies have already been seen in the 1960s and 1970s in some countries, states and districts, and have already generated an awareness of the tensions between decentralisation and centralisation initiatives and the importance of these tensions in the understanding of educational change, which we continue with in our next section.

THE CENTRALISATION–DECENTRALISATION PARADOX AND THE PATHOLOGY OF EDUCATIONAL CHANGE

It has already been noted that, over the past ten years, there has in many countries been a tremendous increase in the amount of change expected of schools. This increase in expectations has been accompanied by fundamental changes in the way schools are managed and governed. In most Western countries there appear to be seemingly contradictory pressures for centralisation (increasing government control over policy and direction) on the one hand, and decentralisation (more responsibility for implementation, resource management and evaluation at the local level) on the other. This tension is making it very difficult for schools and local authorities to implement successfully innovations that make a real difference to the quality of schooling and pupil achievement. The key challenge, as a recent OECD report makes clear, is to find a balance between the increasing demands for centrally determined policy initiatives and quality control, and the encouragement of locally developed school improvement efforts. Three principal conclusions emerge from this report on 'Decentralisation and School Improvement' (OECD, 1989):

- The decentralisation of decision-making as part of school improvement establishes new roles and responsibilities for senior education officials at the centre and for school leaders, teachers and parents at the school level. As new roles are assumed, tensions inevitably develop. Approaches need to be put in place to respond to these tensions.
- Shifts of responsibility to the school level raise the possibility that some functions, formerly carried out at the centre, will not be effectively performed. Central authorities need to ensure, through guidance and support for pre-service, in-service, and community-based programmes, that those assuming new roles have developed the capacity to meet their new responsibilities. External support for schools, reoriented to meet specific school-defined needs, must also be sustained (even if the services are no longer provided by central authorities).
- The management of change, whether at the centre or at the school level, requires a strategy which considers change as a dynamic and evolutionary process. Following on from a clear vision of the expected results of the change, the strategy should anticipate tensions and difficulties but also allow for adaptations and adjustments as the change proceeds.

This type of analysis raises a number of questions about exactly how central policy can be implemented and monitored, while still leaving some latitude for professional judgement at the school level; in particular, about the role of external support, the allocation of resources and the involvement of governors and parents. A general response to the dilemma of decentralisation has been to give more responsibility to schools for their own management. Although this goes by different names in different countries – 'local management of schools', in Britain; 'self managing schools', in Australia; 'site based management' or 'restructuring', in the USA – the concept remains similar. In all cases the school is seen as the unit of change.

Precursors that accentuated the notion of the school as the unit of change are the 'creative school' (Nisbet, 1973); the 'problem solving school' (Bolam, 1982); 'the autonomous school' (van Velzen *et al.*, 1979) and the conceptions of ISIP (which started in 1982). These conceptions are not always associated with clear aims and clearly defined responsibilities, and in the political context there often seems to be contradictory expectations (see, for example, Weiler, 1990; Clune, 1993).

Many of the policies seem to be either politically or ideologically inspired, or an *ad hoc* response to an immediate 'crisis' situation. Simple changes of bureaucratic procedures, or the holding of people more accountable, does not by itself improve the quality of education.

To take the various societies where these policies are being developed in turn, the policies for the 'Local Management of Schools' in England and Wales in the late 1980s were designed to increase the autonomy of schools in their financial arrangements and governance. In general this led to a weakening of the traditional ties between the Local Education Authorities and their schools. Financial delegation, the increased role of governors in the running of the school, and 'opting out' have proven very popular with some, but their benefits upon educational quality are still to be demonstrated.

The phrase the 'Self Managing School' emerged in Tasmania and Victoria, Australia, in the mid-1980s, and has been adapted and emulated in many other school systems, most notably in Edmonton, Alberta, and in many areas of England (Caldwell and Spinks, 1988). This approach was developed initially as a response to the devolution of financial resources to the school level, which by itself is no guarantee of school improvement. The aspirations of this approach can only be achieved if financial plans reflect educational plans, and if resources are allocated to support the priorities that a school has set itself.

In a similar way, current approaches to 'Restructuring' in the USA are attempting a more fundamental approach to educational reform by transforming the organisation of the school in the quest for enhanced student achievement. The restructuring movement in the USA provides perhaps the best and most researched example of the potential and pitfalls of this ubiquitous approach to educational reform. The studies so far conducted suggest that simply devolving budgets or broadening the governance of schools is no guarantee of school improvement (David, 1989; Levine and Eubanks, 1989). Like many other initiatives, restructuring appears superficially attractive and provides a useful banner under which to rally the disparate groups, especially those who know what they dislike about the current ways of organising schools. However, the capacity of restructuring to affect the 'deep structure' of school is currently unclear.

Elmore (1990) suggests that there are three commonly agreed components to restructuring:

- changing the way teaching and learning occurs in schools;
- changing the organisation and internal features of schools (the 'workplace conditions');
- changing the distribution of power between the school and its clients.

Unless these three occur simultaneously, so Elmore's argument goes, there is little likelihood of marked improvements in student outcomes or achievement of the core goals of school. These components of restructuring seem to have some general validity, yet of course they are rarely given much credence in national policies, which are dominated by 'top-down' approaches to change.

A useful definition of the concept of 'restructuring' has been presented by Sashkin and Egermeier (1992: 3): 'Restructuring involves changes in roles, rules, and relationships between and among students and teachers, teachers and administrators, and administrators at various levels from the school building to the district office to the state level, all with the aim of improving student outcomes'. The authors outline four components of successful restructuring; these are: the necessity to decentralise authority; a basic change in accountability; more student focused and less teacher-centred instruction; and the development of new forms of testing that fit the curriculum and the methods of instruction. Yet it is clear that centrally imposed change finds it hard to address the need for these changes, and it is almost always the case that centrally imposed (or 'top-down') change implicitly assumes that implementation is an event rather than a process.

This pathology of policy implementation has recently been described by McLaughlin (1990) in her re-analysis of the large scale 'Rand Change Agent' study undertaken in the USA in the mid–late 1970s. She found that many of the conclusions from the study still hold true today, and commented that:

> A general finding of the Change Agent study that has become almost a truism is that it is exceedingly difficult for policy to change practice, especially across levels of government. Contrary to the one-to-one relationship assumed to exist between policy and practice, the Change Agent study demonstrated that the nature, amount, and pace of change at the local level was a product of local factors that were largely beyond the control of higher-level policymakers.
>
> (McLaughlin 1990: 12)

According to McLaughlin (1990), this general observation has three specific implications:

- policy cannot mandate what matters;
- implementation dominates outcomes;
- local variability is the rule; uniformity is the exception.

The 'Rand' study also looked at the strategies that promoted educational improvement (McLaughlin 1990). Strategies that were generally effective, especially when used together, were:

- concrete, teacher-specific and extended training;
- classroom assistance from local staff;
- teacher observation of similar projects in other classrooms, schools, or districts;
- regular project meetings that focused on practical issues;
- teacher participation in project decisions;
- local development of project materials;
- principals' participation in training.

According to this analysis, the relationship between 'macro-level policies and micro-level behaviour' is paramount. What is needed is an 'implementation friendly' strategy for educational change. A definition of such a strategy, school improvement, is the focus of the following section.

DEFINING SCHOOL IMPROVEMENT

School improvement approaches to educational change embody the long term goal of moving towards the ideal type of the self renewing school. This obviously implies a very different way of thinking about change than the ubiquitous 'top-down' approach discussed earlier. When the school is regarded as the 'centre' of change, then strategies for change need to take this new perspective into account. This approach that centres on the school is exemplified in the work of the OECD-sponsored International School Improvement Project (ISIP), and in the knowledge that emanated from it (van Velzen *et al.*, 1985; Hopkins, 1987, 1990). School improvement was defined in the ISIP as:

> a systematic, sustained effort aimed at change in learning conditions and other related internal conditions in one or more schools,

with the ultimate aim of accomplishing educational goals more effectively.

(van Velzen *et al.*, 1985)

School improvement as an approach to educational change, therefore, rests on a number of assumptions (van Velzen *et al.*, 1985; Hopkins, 1987, 1990). These are that:

- *the school is the centre of change.* This means that external reforms need to be sensitive to the situation in individual schools, rather than assuming that all schools are the same. It also implies that school improvement efforts need to adopt a 'classroom-exceeding' perspective, without ignoring the classroom.
- *there is a systematic approach to change.* School improvement is a carefully planned and managed process that takes place over a period of several years.
- *the 'internal conditions' of schools are a key focus for change.* These include not only the teaching–learning activities in the school, but also the school's procedures, role allocations and resource uses that support the teaching and learning process.
- *educational goals are accomplished more effectively.* Educational goals reflect the particular mission of a school, and represent what the school itself regards as desirable. This suggests a broader definition of outcomes than student scores on achievement tests, even though for some schools these may be pre-eminent. Schools also serve the more general developmental needs of students, the professional development needs of teachers and the needs of its community.
- *there is a multi-level perspective.* Although the school is the centre of change, it does not act alone. The school is embedded in an educational system that has to work collaboratively if the highest degrees of quality are to be achieved. This means that the roles of teachers, heads, governors, parents, support staff (advisers, higher education consultants) and local authorities should be defined, harnessed and committed to the process of school improvement.
- *implementation strategies are integrated.* This implies a linkage between 'top-down' and 'bottom-up', remembering of course that both approaches can apply at a number of different levels in the system. Ideally, 'top-down' policy provides policy aims, an overall strategy, and operational plans; this is complemented by a 'bottom-up' response involving diagnosis, priority goal setting,

and implementation. The former provides the framework, resources and a menu of alternatives; the latter, the energy and the school-based implementation.
• *there is a drive towards institutionalisation.* Change is only success-ful when it has become part of the natural behaviour of teachers in the school. Implementation by itself is not enough.

It is this philosophy and these approaches that underpinned the ISIP and laid the basis for further thinking and action.

A more recent and succinct definition of school improvement is an 'approach to educational change that enhances student outcomes as well as strengthening the school's capacity for managing change' (Hopkins *et al.*, 1994: 3). Unfortunately, the history of educational innovation is littered with the skeletons of innovations and changes whose implementers failed to recognise this key idea. School im-provement in this idea is concerned, not so much about school improvement, but about the *process* of improving, and indeed part of the problem of centralised educational reform is the preoccupation with outcomes at the expense of the process that leads to such outcomes.

Although the term 'school improvement' is now in common usage, the complexities of the approach as an alternative means of educa-tional change have not necessarily been fully explored. This more rigorous recent definition implies a broader and more sophisticated view of the concept, in which school improvement can be regarded (Hopkins *et al.*, 1994):

• as a vehicle for planned educational change (but also realising that educational change is necessary for school improvement);
• as particularly appropriate during times of centralised initiatives and innovation overload when there are competing reforms to implement;
• as usually necessitating some form of external support;
• as having an emphasis on strategies for strengthening the school's capacity for managing change; while
• raising student achievement (broadly defined); through
• specifically focusing on the teaching–learning process.

THE PROCESS OF CHANGE AND SCHOOL IMPROVEMENT

The literature on planned school change is crucial to the way in which contemporary school improvement strategies are formulated. There is now solid, research-based evidence about how the change process unfolds over time. As Miles (1986) and Fullan (1991) have demonstrated, the change process is not linear, but consists of a series of three stages that can merge into each other. Although these phases often co-exist in practice, there are some advantages in describing them separately; particularly in terms of what happens during them, and in terms of what behaviours within each phase make for success. The process is generally considered to consist of three overlapping phases – initiation, implementation, and institutionalisation.

Although implementation has received the most attention historically, this has most probably been disadvantageous to the understanding of the process as a whole. Emphasising initiation and implementation at the expense of institutionalisation leads to a very short-term view of innovation. Consequently, it is probably more helpful to think of the three phases as a series of overlapping phases, rather than as a straight line.

The *initiation* phase is about deciding to embark on innovation, and about developing commitment towards the process. The key activities in the initiation phase are the decision to start the innovation, and a review of the school's current state as regards the particular innovation. There are, however, a number of factors associated with initiation that will influence whether the change gets started in the first place. These are issues such as the existence of and access to innovations, pressures from within and without the school, the availability of resources and consultancy support, and the quality of the school's internal conditions and organisation. Fullan (1991) describes them in detail and emphasises that it is not simply the existence of these factors but their combination that is important. He describes the following factors as being of importance in determining the quality of the initiation phase:

1 The existence and quality of innovations.
2 Access to innovations.
3 Advocacy from central administration.
4 Teacher advocacy.
5 Presence of external change agents.
6 Community factors (pressure, support, apathy).

7   New policy-funds (federal/state/local).
8   Problem-solving capacities within the school.

Miles (1986) has also made an analysis of the factors that make for successful initiation:

- the innovation should be tied to a local agenda and high profile local need;
- a clear, well-structured approach to change should be present;
- there should be an active advocate or champion who understands the innovation and supports it;
- there should be active initiation to start the innovation ('top-down' initiation can be acceptable under certain conditions);
- the innovation should be of good quality.

Implementation is the phase of the process which has received the most attention. This is the phase of the attempted use of the innovation. Factors influencing implementation are the characteristics of the change, the internal conditions of the school and the pressure and support from outside. It is during this phase that skills and understanding are being acquired, some success may be being achieved, and in which responsibility is delegated to working groups of teachers. It is often helpful to regard implementation as being of two types: pre-implementation and implementation. Many innovations founder at the pre-implementation stage, because not enough initial support has been generated.

The key activities occurring during implementation are the carrying out of action plans, the development and sustaining of commitment, the checking of progress and the overcoming of problems.

Institutionalisation is the phase when innovation and change stop being regarded as something new and become part of the school's 'usual' way of doing things, yet, until recently, it was assumed to happen automatically, despite the evidence that innovations associated with many centralised initiatives tend to fade away after the initial wave of enthusiasm, or after a key actor leaves, or when the funding ceases. The move from implementation to institutionalisation, however, often involves the transformation of a pilot project into a school-wide initiative, often without the advantage of the previously available funding. It is change of a new order and, in these cases, there tends to be widespread use of the change by staff, its impact is seen on classroom practice, and the whole process is no longer regarded as being unusual. As the researchers who worked on the DESSI

(Dissemination Efforts Supporting School Improvement) study remarked (Huberman and Crandall, quoted in Miles, 1983: 14):

> In the chronicle of research on dissemination and use of educational practices, we first put our chips on adoption, then on implementation. It turns out that these investments are lost without deliberate attention to the institutional steps that lock an innovation into the local setting. New practices that get built in to the training, regulatory, staffing and budgetary cycle survive; others don't. Innovations are highly perishable goods. Taking institutionalisation for granted – assuming somewhat magically that it will happen by itself, or will necessarily result from a technically mastered, demonstrably effective project – is naive and usually self-defeating.

Key activities to ensure success at this stage according to Miles (1986) are:

- an emphasis on 'embedding' the change within the school's structures, its organisation and resources;
- the elimination of competing or contradictory practices;
- strong and purposeful links to other change efforts, to the curriculum and to classroom teaching;
- widespread take-up in the school and in the local area;
- an adequate 'bank' of local facilitators and/or advisory teachers for skills training.

A FRAMEWORK FOR SCHOOL IMPROVEMENT

It is possible to divide the concept of school development into a number of constituent factors. Stocktaking the possible factors and variables that influence school development leads to a large list and, for reasons of clarity, it is necessary to order them. This framework is based on Voogt (1986) and on Hopkins (1996).

Figure 4.1 summarises the most important components of school development (for an elaboration, see Lagerweij and Haak, 1994). The framework gives the opportunity to distinguish the different aspects without losing the relations between them. The factors determine the mutual interaction, the capacities and the results of the school. In fact, such a picture is beginning to connect the effectiveness literature with the school improvement literature (Hopkins, 1990; Dimmock, 1993; Cuttance, 1994; Lagerweij and Haak, 1994).

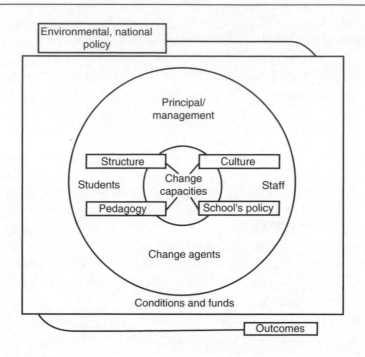

Figure 4.1 A framework for analysing school improvement

In the centre of the framework are the school's capacities to learn. The factors that influence the development of the school also determine the possibility of change: the change capacity. Schools differ greatly in their ability to change (see Rosenholtz, 1989; van Gennip, 1991; Fullan, 1992; Cuttance 1994; Louis and Kruse, 1995; Stoll and Fink, 1996), and an explanation for these differences can be found in the different stages of development of the many components within the school.

In the framework, it is clear that a dynamic interaction is concerned here. Ten factors are distinguished. School improvement presupposes the involvement of many different groups at different levels: the teachers, the school leader, the change agents and other support people, and the students). Each factor contains building blocks for the change-capacities of the organisation as a whole:

1 The innovation policy of the school.

2 The interventions of the school leader, internal and external support.
3 The organisational structure of the school.
4 The school culture.
5 The educational organisation of the school (curriculum and pedagogy).
6 The members of the team, their values and concerns.
7 The students, their background and their levels of development.
8 The student results, the output.
9 The school at local and national level.
10 The conditions, means and facilities.

The change capacities are at the centre of the diagram. Based on a number of empirical studies, it seems that the factors that determine the change capacities of a school can be divided into four groups:

• *Capacities of the school leaders*   Leadership and management are important in organisations. The school leader has to show capacities as functioning as a leader and innovator, being able to tell how changes can be applied in practice, being able to determine the scope of change, the capacity of support and stimulation, and being able to develop skills to foster a learning organisation (Vandenberghe and van der Vegt, 1992; Louis and Kruse, 1995). Very often the expression 'educational leadership' is used to describe this collection of attributes (Levine and Lezotte, 1990; Louis and Miles, 1990; Fullan, 1991; Kruger, 1994; Murphy and Louis, 1994; Leithwood and Steinback, 1995; Leithwood, 1995).

• *Communication and decision making*   In the execution of tasks, many decisions and rules have to be made. Spreading this information and those procedures so that they can be utilised can be seen as part of the professional school culture (Vandenberghe, 1993a), along with staff meetings, collective decision-making, staff being able to discuss conflicts of interest, and good professional relations between members of the team (see Fullan, 1992, Campo, 1993; Scheerens, 1994).

• *Process planning and evaluation*   Planning and evaluation can contribute to the development of policies in the school. This concerns the establishment of plans, the distribution of tasks, the recognition of blocks on change, and the evaluation of the progress of the process of change (Louis and Miles, 1990; Sleegers, 1991; Vandenberghe and van der Vegt, 1992).

* *Coordination in the school organisation*   This concept is elaborated by Mintzberg (1990, 1992). He discerns the importance of 'co-ordination-mechanisms' such as mutual adjustment, direct supervision, the standardisation of work processes, standardisation of output, standardisation of skills and knowledge, and the generation of cohesive ideology). In the school, these factors are visible in, for example, the leadership styles, the regulation and evaluation of the curriculum, the procedures for the grouping of students and teachers, and the assignment of problem-solving teams (see Hofman and Lugthart, 1991; Henkin and Wanat, 1994; Witziers, 1992).

Besides these capacities which are important for the entire organisation, there are three 'mechanisms' which also play an important role, and which we extract from the works of Mintzberg (1990, 1992). To create space for policy at school level, the mechanisms can be regarded as characterising the school as an organisation (see Leithwood, 1995; Louis and Kruse, 1995; Hopkins *et al.*, 1994). These mechanisms are *vision*, *planning*, and *learning*.

Vision guides a policy or a development process in a particular direction. It is the answer to the question, 'Where do we want to go?' Although schools are embedded in a national framework of legislation, each school is free, to an extent, to give shape to its own educational vision.

These popularly entitled 'mission statements' reflect a school's vision on education. They highlight what the school regards as important, the core aims of the school's teaching. 'Vision', with respect to educational change, can thus be defined as a normative ideal of a desirable future, which is both inspiring and challenging, has a built-in commitment of almost all those involved, and which encourages educational change. Vision can be the moving spirit behind educational change. It is therefore important that all those involved play a part in the development and continuance of a vision. If the school management, as well as the teachers, parents and students, contribute from their respective viewpoints, everyone will have a feeling that his/her own vision is in line with the common vision. This can be inspiring and encouraging. A commonly shared vision has, therefore, a considerable effect on the efficacy of the implementation of innovations.

Planning is a methodical way of working, as well as a systematic coordination of the activities, and is the key to successful school development. Reality, however, is not wholly manageable, and schools do not always work on educational change on a systematic basis. In general, they casually try *ad hoc* changes before systematising them. Besides, schools often don't exclusively operate on a rational basis – psychological and emotional factors also play a role. The assumption that the entire school development process can be rationally planned is, therefore, something of a myth, and there are numerous unpredictable circumstances and sudden events that play havoc with any over-rigorous planning scheme.

However, the systematising and codifying of priorities that is the purpose of planning can greatly aid school change (Hargreaves and Hopkins, 1991).

Learning is the mechanism that gives the organisation and the people involved in it the chance to learn the new skills and insights that are needed. Teachers in an innovative school are aware of the fact that they are learning too. In many cases it can be a new experience for teachers to cooperate with their colleagues, because they are used only to the isolation of their classrooms. They actually have to *learn* to work together.

Thus, training of the individual teacher and the entire teaching staff is an important and indispensable feature in school development. Since it is the people (the members of the staff) who collectively determine the quality of the school as an organisation, learning is obviously an indispensable characteristic of the school organisation. The innovative school is a learning organisation.

STRATEGIES FOR CHANGE

It has already been argued that external policy initiatives are *not* by themselves a sufficient strategy for school improvement, and that strategies that are internal to the school, such as school review or evaluation, development planning and staff development, have to be adopted. We have further suggested that, if change is to have any significant impact upon student achievement, such strategies need to be integrated at the school level. Such integration provides an infrastructure for change that can support the necessary developments in teaching and classroom practice that we know to have a positive effect on the progress of students.

The striking conclusion that we have noted from studies of policy implementation is that, although policies set directions and provide a framework, they do not and cannot determine outcomes. It is implementation, rather than the decision to adopt a new policy, that determines student achievement. It is also the case that the most effective school improvement strategies seem to be those that are internal, rather than external, to the school. Three of the most common 'internal' school improvement programmes, school self review/evaluation, development planning, and staff development, are now briefly described.

Since the early 1980s, and for a variety of reasons, *school self evaluation or school based review* (SBR) has been regarded as a strategy that could not only strengthen the capacity of the school to develop and renew itself, but also provide both evidence for accountability purposes and a structure for managing the change process. The OECD International School Improvement Project (ISIP), in particular, took a leading role in conceptualising and disseminating examples of various schemes for school-based review (see Bollen and Hopkins, 1987; Hopkins, 1988). The three examples given below represent the 'state of the art' of school self evaluation when it was most popular:

- The Schools Council *Guidelines for Internal Review and Development* (GRIDS) project was designed to help teachers review and develop the curriculum and organisation of their school, and two practical handbooks, one primary, one secondary, were produced for the purpose (Abbott *et al.*, 1988).
- The *Institutional Development Programme* (IDP) originated within IMTEC (The International Movement Towards Educational Change), as a result of international collaboration which began in Norway in 1974. The IDP was based on a survey feedback design with the emphasis being placed on use of a standardised questionnaire, consultant support and a systematic feedback-development process (Dalin and Rust, 1983).
- The *Systematic Analysis for School Improvement* (SAS) project was based at the Department of Education of the University of Utrecht. The SAS is essentially a diagnostic instrument for the linking of the school's organisation to staff development and school improvement (Voogt, 1989).

During the 1980s, school-based review/evaluation, despite confusion over its purposes, established itself as a major strategy for managing the change process and institutional renewal. The empirical support for its utility, however, is at best ambivalent (see, for example, Clift *et al.*, 1987). For most schools it has proven easier to identify priorities for future development than to implement selected changes within a specific timeframe. Because of this, and the failure to implement the total process, for example, of training for feedback and follow up, SBR has had, despite its popularity, limited impact on the effectiveness of schools.

As the pace of change quickened in the late 1980s, more effective and comprehensive strategies for school improvement were sought. One of the best known and widely used 'meta-strategies' for school improvement in Western educational systems has been *development planning*. This approach ('school growth plans' is another term) provides a generic and paradigmatic illustration of a school improvement strategy, combining as it does selected curriculum change with modifications to the school's management arrangements or organisation. As compared with school review, where evaluation is the initial step in the cycle, development planning emphasises evaluation occurring, often in different forms, throughout the process.

Development planning is a strategy that is becoming increasingly widespread in British schools, for example, as teachers and school leaders struggle to take control of the process of change. The DES project in England and Wales on *School Development Plans* (SDP) is a good illustration of an attempt to develop a strategy that would, among other things, help governors, heads and staff to change the culture of their school (Hargreaves and Hopkins, 1991).

This brief review of evaluation and planning strategies for school improvement has been descriptive rather than critical. Now is the time to ask the crucial question, 'What link is there between these strategies and student achievement?' The simple answer is that these strategies can and do create the conditions for enhanced student achievement, but by themselves have little direct impact on the progress of pupils. In all of the examples given so far, self evaluation and planning efforts were creating the conditions for curriculum and instructional change. They are necessary, but not *sufficient*, conditions for enhancing student achievement. They have to be integrated with, or lead to, specific modifications in curriculum or teaching if the result is to be enhanced student outcomes (Joyce and Showers 1988). The key strategy for achieving this is clearly in-service training (INSET) or staff development.

The research evidence that is available on the effectiveness of staff development initiatives is, however, far from encouraging. Despite all the efforts and resources that have been utilised, the impact of such programmes in terms of improvements in learning outcomes for students is rather disappointing (Fullan, 1991). Joyce and Showers' (1988) work on staff development, and in particular their peer coaching strategy, has in recent years, however, transformed thinking about what is necessary to ensure effective staff development. Joyce and Showers have identified a number of key training components which, when used in combination, have much greater power than when they have been used alone. The major components of such effective training are:

- Presentation of theory and description of skill or strategy;
- Modelling or demonstration of the skills or models of teaching;
- Practice in simulated and classroom settings;
- Structured and open-ended feedback (provision of information about performance);
- Coaching for direct application (hands-on, in-classroom assistance with the transfer of skills and strategies to the classroom).

More recently, Joyce (1996) has distinguished between the two key elements of staff development: the workshop and the workplace. The *workshop*, which is equivalent to best practice on the traditional INSET course, is where we gain understanding, see demonstrations of the teaching strategy we may wish to acquire, and have the opportunity to practise them in a non-threatening environment. If, however, we wish to transfer those skills that the workshop has introduced us to back into the *workplace* – the classroom and school – then merely attending the workshop is insufficient. The research evidence is very clear that skill acquisition and the ability to transfer vertically to a range of situations requires 'on-the-job-support'. This implies changes to the organisation of the workplace and to the way in which we organise staff development in our schools. In particular this means introducing the opportunity for immediate and sustained practise, collaboration and peer coaching, and for studying development and implementation. We cannot achieve these changes in the workplace without, in most cases, drastic alterations in the ways in which we organise our schools, yet we will not be able to transfer teaching skills from INSET sessions to a range of classrooms without them. Successful schools clearly pay careful attention to their workplace conditions.

It is now important to summarise this discussion on the three 'internal' programmes for school improvement. In many countries, schools are faced with a number of innovations – self evaluation, development planning, changes in staff development policy and practice – that are 'content free'. Although they all have a carefully specified process or structure, the substance of each is for the teacher and school to decide. In combination, these strategies can form an 'infrastructure' at the school level that facilitates the implementation of specific curriculum changes and/or teaching methods that can have a direct impact upon student achievement.

This multi-dimensional view of school improvement is well captured in Joyce's (1991) review of a series of individual innovations, which he describes as being 'doors' which can open or unlock the process of school improvement. Joyce concludes that each approach emphasises different aspects of school culture at the outset – in other words, they provide a range of ways of 'getting into' school improvement. Each door opens a passageway into the culture of the school. His review (Joyce, 1991) reveals five major emphases:

1 Collegiality: the developing of collaborative and professional relations within a school staff and between their surrounding communities.
2 Research: where a school staff studies research findings about, for example, effective school and teaching practices, or the process of change.
3 Action Research: teachers collecting and analysing information and data about their classrooms and schools, and their students' progress.
4 Curriculum Initiatives: the introduction of changes within subject areas or, as in the case of the computer, across curriculum areas.   ·
5 Teaching Strategies: when teachers discuss, observe and acquire a range of teaching skills and strategies.

He argues that all these emphases can eventually change the culture of an individual school substantially. If each door to school improvement is carefully examined, one can discover where each is likely to lead, how the passageways are connected, what proponents of any one approach can borrow from the others, and the costs and benefits of opening any one (or any combination). Joyce argues that single approaches are unlikely to be as powerful an agent for school improvement as a multiple strategy.

The implicit assumption made by Joyce is that 'behind the door' are a series of interconnecting pathways that lead inexorably to school improvement, but unfortunately this is not always so. Because of their singular nature, most school improvement strategies, as we have seen, fail to a greater or lesser degree to effect the culture of the school. They tend to focus on individual changes, and individual teachers and classrooms, rather than upon how these changes can fit in with and adapt the organisation and ethos of the school. As a consequence, when the door is opened it only leads into a cul-de-sac, which partially accounts for the uneven effect of most educational reforms.

SOME PROPOSITIONS FOR SUCCESSFUL SCHOOL IMPROVEMENT

The failure of many efforts towards change to progress beyond early implementation is partially explained by the lack of realisation on the part of those involved about the importance of vision, planning and learning, and the lack of awareness that each of the phases of school improvement have different characteristics and require different strategies if success is to be achieved (Cuttance, 1994). It is the general knowledge about the way in which the change or school improvement process unfolds, described in previous sections, that lays the basis for considering the following more specific propositions concerning the practice of school improvement (Hopkins *et al.*, 1996).

Proposition One – Without a clear focus on the internal conditions of the school, improvement efforts quickly become marginalised

There is no one-to-one relationship between policy and implementation, and one of the great fallacies of educational change is that policy directives, from any level, have a direct impact on student achievement. What is known from experience, as well as from the research on student achievement and school effectiveness, is that the greatest impact upon student progress is achieved by those innovations or adaptations of practice that intervene in, or modify, the learning process. Changes in classroom factors, such as curriculum, teaching methods, grouping practices and assessment procedures, have the greatest potential impact on the performance of students. Having said this, there is still a debate, acrimonious at times, as to which curriculum, which teaching methods, which grouping arrangements, and which assessment procedures, best serve the progress of students. These are important issues the resolution of which is beyond the scope of this particular chapter. Suffice it to say that these issues are best addressed through reflection on good practice and the interrogation of research, rather than being informed by the dogma of politicians and their ideologically inspired advisers!

Two points have been made so far: the first is that policy directives do not *directly* effect the progress of students; the second, that it is changes in *classroom* practice that most directly effect student learning. The main point, however, is that school improvement works best when a clear and practical focus for development based upon these two insights is linked to simultaneous work on the internal conditions within the school. Conditions are the internal features of the school, the 'arrangements' that enable it to get work done. Without an equal focus on these conditions, even developmental priorities that directly affect classroom practice quickly become marginalised.

Within the IQEA (Improving the Quality of Education for ALL) project (see Chapter 6, and Hopkins *et al.*, 1994), for example, a number of 'conditions' within the school have been seen as being associated with its capacity for sustained development. At present, the best estimate of these conditions which underpin improvement efforts can be broadly stated as:

- a commitment to *staff development*;
- practical efforts to *involve* staff, students and the community in school policies and decisions;
- 'transformational' *leadership* approaches that increase 'the lateral drift' of decision making;
- effective *coordination* strategies;
- proper attention to the potential benefits of *enquiry and reflection*;
- a commitment to *collaborative planning* activity.

What is of central importance to the argument here is that, if there is a full commitment to the improvement of pupil outcomes, then work on the internal conditions of the school has to complement development priorities related to classroom practice.

Proposition Two – School improvement will not occur unless clear decisions are made about development and maintenance

It is all well and good to talk about development in broad terms, but, given current concerns about overload in our change-rich environment, such a general and unfocused agenda is unrealistic. Decisions need to be made about *what* changes need to be implemented and *how* they are to be selected. This is a profound question, and one that reflects what is perhaps the most crucial challenge facing schools today – how to balance both change and stability effectively, how on the one hand to preserve what is already admirable and fine in a school, and on the other, how to respond positively to innovation and the challenge of change.

Bearing this conundrum in mind, the distinction was introduced in *The Empowered School* (Hargreaves and Hopkins 1991), between a school's development and its maintenance activities. Maintenance refers to the carrying out of the school's day-to-day activities, to the fulfilling of its statutory obligations, and to delivering the curriculum to the best of its ability. Development, on the other hand, refers to that amount of resource, time and energy the school reserves from the total it has available for carrying forward those aims, aspirations and activities that 'add value' to what it already does. It is through its development activities that a school continues to make progress in times of change.

The effective use of those resources devoted to development obviously implies a high level of prioritisation. Michael Fullan once described it as: 'Do one thing as well as you possibly can, and do everything else as well as you would have done anyway'. A common problem is that many schools overload their development plans and, because there is insufficient distinction between plans for development and plans for maintenance (e.g. those devoted to budgets, timetable, staffing), there is a tendency to put all external changes into development, thus ensuring that nothing gets done properly. The conceptual distinction between development and maintenance should allow the school to make more coherent decisions about what it is to devote its developmental energy to, irrespective to some extent of the needs of the external reform agenda.

There is also evidence that the most successful schools are deliberately creating contrasting but mutually supportive structural arrangements to cope with the twin pressures of development and maintenance. Schools are finding out quite rapidly, or eventually more painfully, that maintenance structures established to organise teaching, learning and assessment, cannot also cope with developmental activities which inevitably cut across established hierarchies, curriculum areas, meeting patterns, and timetables. The innovative responses required for sustained development, e.g. delegation, task groups, high levels of specific staff development, quality time for planning and collaborative classroom activity, are inimical to successful maintenance. What is required are complementary structures, each with their own purpose, budget and ways of working. Obviously the majority of a school's time and resources will go on maintenance but, unless there is also an element dedicated to development, then the school is unlikely to progress in times of change.

Proposition Three – Successful school improvement involves adapting external change for internal purposes

The distinction between development and maintenance relates to development planning. Development planning itself is commonly regarded as an important preliminary to school improvement. The planning cycle is likely to involve the school in generating a number of 'priorities' for action – often too many to work on. This means that decisions about 'priorities' must be made – moving from the separate, perhaps even conflicting, priorities of individuals or groups to a systematically compiled set of priorities which represents the overall needs of a whole school community. Two principles should guide this process of choice amongst priorities (Hargreaves and Hopkins, 1991):

- *manageability* – how much can we realistically hope to achieve?
- *coherence* – is there a sequence which will ease implementation?

To these principles a third should be added:

- *consonance* – the extent to which internally identified priorities coincide or overlap with external pressures for reform.

There is empirical evidence to suggest that those schools which recognise *consonance*, and therefore see externally generated change efforts as providing opportunities, as well as (or instead of) problems, are better able to respond to external demands. It is through such an attitude towards planning that schools begin to see the potential in adapting external change to internal purpose.

Most schools quite logically regard the sequence just described as the appropriate way to plan their school improvement activities, and in many ways it is. Some schools, however, and those that appear to be more successful than most at managing school improvement, begin at the other end of the sequence – with student learning goals. It is as if they say, 'what changes in student performance do we wish to see this year?' Having decided that, they then devise a strategy for so doing, and establish a priority which they can link to some external change, preferably one that has resources attached to it! It is in this way that the most successful schools pursue their improvement efforts, through adapting external change for internal purpose.

Proposition Four – Educational change should be based principally on the school as a unit, and on the teacher as the pivot in the change process

The notion of the 'school as a unit' relates to the school's capacity to initiate innovations and bring them to a favourable conclusion, which presupposes a set of characteristics and skills, both at organisational and at individual level. Very often, innovations have to be implemented at classroom level. The secondary processes at the organisational level shape the conditions for the implementation processes at micro (classroom) level.

One of the criticisms of school improvement efforts is that, despite their often grand aspirations, they are in reality only a façade for simple and low level staff development. Successful school improvement work is underpinned, therefore, with a *contract* between the partners, which defines the parameters of the project and the obligations of those involved to each other, and which is intended to clarify expectations and ensure the climate necessary for success. In particular, such a contract should emphasise that all staff be consulted, that coordinators are appointed, that a 'critical mass' of teachers is actively involved in development work, and that sufficient time is made available for classroom observation and staff development.

It is also important that school improvement should affect all 'levels' of the school, since one of the things that we know from research and experience is that change will not be successful unless it impacts all levels of the organisation. Specifically the focus is on the three levels outlined in Figure 4.2, and on integrating the levels and the ways in which these interrelate. The senior team level is responsible for overall management and the establishment of policies, particularly with respect to how resources and strategies for staff development can be mobilised in support of school improvement efforts. The department or working group level comprises those established groups within the school responsible for curriculum, teaching and learning. Finally, at the individual teacher level, the focus is on developing classroom practice and the teachers' own professional development.

In very effective schools, these three levels are mutually supportive.

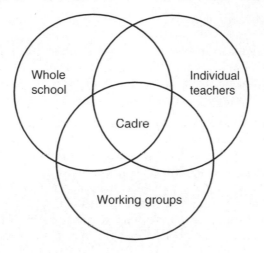

Figure 4.2 The three levels of school improvement

Consequently, a specific aim of school improvement strategies should be to devise and establish positive conditions at each level, and to coordinate support across these levels.

Proposition Five – Data about the school's performance creates the energy for development

Those schools which recognise that enquiry into and reflection on the school's performance are important elements within the improvement process possess additional momentum for change. This seems to be particularly true where there is widespread staff involvement in these processes, and when there are good reasons for such participation. For example, it is much easier to focus efforts around the school's priorities when every member of staff sees him or herself as playing a role in the evaluation of the related policies and practices. Similarly, it is often only teachers who possess vital knowledge about classroom outcomes, so any attempt to evaluate on the basis of a senior manager's perceptions is at best partial. As Ainscow and his colleagues have suggested (Ainscow *et al.*, 1994: 12), enquiry and reflection as developmental 'tools' are at their most effective when there is:

- systematic collection, interpretation and use of school-generated data in decision-making;

- an effective strategy for reviewing the progress and impact of school policies and initiatives;
- widespread staff involvement in the processes of data collection and analysis;
- a clearly established set of 'ground rules' for the collection, control and use of school generated data.

The need to ground policy decisions in data about how the school is functioning is paramount. Too often, elaborate policy-making processes are set up to validate the directions and priorities which school managers favour, rather than identify what is actually appropriate for the particular school. Of course, there is also a feedback role to be filled by data gathering to determine whether or not policies are having impact in the areas they seek to address. But here the focus needs to remain on the collection of evidence on impact, and not merely of implementation. It is vital to keep this distinction in mind. It is too easy to convince oneself that the school is being improved while, in reality, all that is occurring is a change in policies. Involving teachers in this process also provides them with a stimulus to make changes work for the benefit of students.

Proposition Six – Successful school improvement efforts engender a language about teaching and change

Taken together, these propositions are highly consistent with Joyce's analysis of the characteristics of effective large-scale school improvement initiatives (Joyce *et al.*, 1993: 72), in so far as these have tended to:

- focus on specific outcomes which can be related to student learning, rather than adopt laudable but non-specific goals such as 'improve exam results';
- draw on theory, research into practice and the teachers' own experience in formulating strategies, so that a rationale for the required changes is established in the minds of those expected to bring them about;
- target staff development, since it is unlikely that developments in student learning will occur without developments in teachers' practice;
- monitor the impact of policy on practice early and regularly, rather than rely on *post-hoc* evaluation.

There are two respects in which these characteristics are particularly relevant to the theme of this chapter. First, they provide an example of how the priority for development (the first two points) links together with simultaneous work on the school conditions (the second two points). This marriage is a vital component of sustainable improvement efforts.

Second is the emphasis on specifications of teaching and learning. All too often in recent years, the focus of educational changes has centred on curriculum contents rather than curriculum processes. Though this emphasis is understandable, given the enormous pressure the National Curriculum in England and Wales, for example, has exerted on curriculum planning, it is nevertheless unfortunate. Unfortunate because, in a situation where curricula are being increasingly imposed by central authorities, there is still the opportunity for teachers to be creative in their use of teaching strategies. Moreover, there is mounting evidence that the content of a lesson notwithstanding, the use of appropriate teaching strategies can dramatically increase student achievement (Joyce *et al.*, 1996). A major goal for school improvement, therefore, is to help teachers become professionally flexible so that they can select, from a repertoire of possibilities, the teaching approach most suited to their particular content area, and the age, interests and aptitudes of their students.

It is our firm belief that one of the characteristics of successful schools is that *teachers talk about teaching*. There is a growing literature about classroom practice to help focus such discussions (see, for example: Joyce *et al.*, 1996; Creemers, 1994; Hopkins *et al.*, 1994; Hopkins and Stern, 1996). The research on teaching approaches can help to initiate the dialogue. The very existence of a vocabulary both facilitates sharing and empowers practice. At the heart of this empowerment are a number of activities which we have found to be helpful. These include:

- teachers discussing with each other the nature of teaching strategies;
- establishing specifications or guidelines for the chosen teaching strategies;
- agreeing on standards used to assess student progress as a result;
- mutual observation and partnership teaching in the classroom.

It is in this way, as Judith Little once remarked, that 'teachers teach each other the practice of teaching'.

TOWARDS A THEORY FOR SCHOOL IMPROVEMENT

Although it is inappropriate to draw conclusions from an exploratory chapter such as this, the discussion does raise a series of questions that need to be debated, and suggests a broad agenda for research, policy and practice in the area of school improvement.

Our discussion on the *effectiveness of school improvement initiatives* was informed by a series of questions about how the process of school development is best facilitated. Is the presence of a centralised reform agenda in most Western countries a sufficient strategy for school improvement? Is school development a naturally occurring phenomenon? Or does it require some form of external support? If it does, are different support strategies required for different schools at different stages of development? These are the sorts of questions that come to mind when thinking about school improvement strategies.

As regards needed *research*, there is one general exhortation and two suggestions. The exhortation is that, in the area of school improvement, we have for too long been content with anecdotal evidence and perceptual data collected unsystematically. If the field is to be true to its rhetoric, then serious questions must be asked about theory and strategy, which must also be tested empirically. As to the suggestions, the first is to call for the need to develop experimental (or, in the argot of the discipline, quasi-experimental) designs for educational research, in this case the effectiveness of school improvement interventions. In particular, it is important to track the relationship between 'independent' or process variables, and 'dependent' or outcome variables, in the school improvement field (Hopkins, 1995). The second suggestion is to develop methodologies for exploring the process of change in schools. At present the range of research methods open to those who take school improvement seriously is very limited, and much more work needs to be done in this area. The Cambridge school improvement group has recently made a small contribution to this endeavour by developing six innovative techniques for 'mapping the process of change in schools (Cambridge University, 1994; Ainscow *et al.*, 1995).

There are two suggestions as regards *policy*. Neither are original, but both are profound. The first is to incorporate within policy some of the insights developed from the work on school change, school effectiveness and improvement, all of which regard change as 'more of a process than an event'. Although this sounds trite, if politicians had taken this suggestion seriously the current 'era' of reform might perhaps by now be producing unequivocally positive results. The second suggestion is to re-centre the discussion of innovation and reform upon student outcomes. Unless this is done, the whole debate on educational change, school improvement and social equity will remain ideological, semantic and vacuous. Recent methods for evaluating school effectiveness and pupil progress, using authentic assessment (see, for example, the work of Peter Hill and his colleagues at the University of Melbourne: Rowe *et al.*, 1993) and meta-analysis techniques which allow us some operational purchase on the 'effect size' of various strategies for improvement (for a discussion of how this applies to teaching models, see Joyce and Weil, 1996) would, if they became part of the public debate, fundamentally transform the ways in which we as a society view education.

Finally, *practice*. There are two practical issues which complement and overlap the previous suggestions on research and policy. The first is to become more clear in an operational sense about what school improvement actually is, and to clarify the distinction between 'naturally occurring', 'internally driven' and 'externally supported' school improvement. Second, to become far more sensitive to the 'growth states' or 'performance cycles' of schools (Cuttance, 1994). For example, do failing schools respond in different ways to school improvement initiatives than more successful schools? This notion of the potential importance of context specificity in the precise improvement strategies chosen is something we return to in Chapter 6.

More clarity on these three sets of issues would go a long way to transforming the image of school improvement as just another form of staff development, and of school improvement researchers and practitioners as those who only commit 'random acts of kindness', as one commentator recently put it. It would also give school improvement research and development the maturity to enter into full and mutually supportive partnership with those working within the school effectiveness tradition, a partnership which would have the mutually beneficial effects that we outline in the next chapter.

REFERENCES

Abbott, R., Birchenough, M. and Steadman, S. (1988) *GRIDS School Handbooks*, (Second Edition, Primary and Secondary versions), York: Longman for the SCDC.

Ainscow, M., Hargreaves, D. H. and Hopkins, D. (1995) 'Mapping the process of change in schools', *Evaluation and Research in Education*, 9(2), 75–90.

Ainscow, M., Hopkins, D., Southworth, G. and West, M. (1994) *Creating the Conditions for School Improvement*, London: David Fulton.

Bolam, R. (1982) *Strategies for School Improvement*. Report for the Organization for Economic Co-operation and Development, University of Bristol.

Bollen, R. and Hopkins, D. (1987) *School Based Review: Towards a Praxis*, Leuven: ACCO.

Caldwell, B. and Spinks, J. (1988) *The Self Managing School*, London: Falmer Press.

Cambridge University (1994) *Mapping Change in Schools – The Cambridge Manual of Research Techniques*, Cambridge: University of Cambridge Institute of Education.

Campo, C. (1993) *Collaborative School Cultures: How principles can make a difference*, San Francisco: Jossey-Bass.

Clift, P. and Nuttall, D. (1987) *Studies in School Self Evaluation*, Lewes: Falmer Press.

Clune, W. H. (1993) 'The best path to systemic educational policy: Standard/centralized or differentiated/decentralized?', *Educational Evaluation and Policy Analysis*, 15, 233–54.

Crandall, D, Eiseman, J. and Louis, K. S. (1986) 'Strategic planning issues that bear on the success of school improvement efforts', *Educational Administration Quarterly*, 22(2), 21–53.

Crandall, D. and others (1982) *People, Policies and Practice: Examining the Chain of School Improvement*, (vols 1–10), Andover, MA: The Network.

Creemers, B. (1994) *The Effective Classroom*, London: Cassell.

Cuttance, P. (1994) *Quality Systems for the Performance Development Cycle of Schools*. Paper prepared for the International Conference for School Effectiveness and Improvement, Sydney: New South Wales Department of School Education.

Dalin, P. and Rust, V. (1983) *Can Schools Learn?*, Windsor: NFER Nelson.

David, J. (1989) 'Synthesis of learning on school based management', *Educational Leadership*, 48(8), 45–53.

Dimmock, C. (ed.) (1993) *Schoolbased Management and School Effectiveness*, London: Routledge.

Elmore, R. (1990) *Restructuring Schools*, Oakland, CA: Jossey-Bass.

Fullan, M. (1985) 'Change processes and strategies at the local level', *The Elementary School Journal*, 85(3), 391–421.

—— (1991) *The New Meaning of Educational Change*, London/New York: Cassell.

—— (1992) *Successful School Improvement*, Buckingham/Philadelphia: Open University Press.

—— (1993) *Change Forces. Probing the Depths of Educational Reform*, London/New York/Philadelphia: Falmer Press.

Gennip, J. van (1991) *Veranderingscapaciteiten van basisscholen*, Nijmegen: ITS.

Hargreaves, D. H. (Chair) (1984) *Improving Secondary Schools*, London: ILEA.

Hargreaves, D. H. and Hopkins, D. (1991) *The Empowered School*, London: Cassell.

Henkin, A. B. and Wanat, C. L. (1994) 'Problem-solving teams and the improvement of organizational preformance in schools', *School Organization*, 14(2), 121–39.

Hofman, R. H. and Lugthart, E. (1991) *Interne capaciteiten in het voortgezet onderwijs*, Groningen: RION.

Hopkins, D. (ed.) (1987) *Improving the Quality of Schooling*, London: Falmer Press.

——(1988) *Doing School Based Review*, Leuven: ACCO.

—— (1990) 'The international school improvement project (ISIP) and effective schooling: Towards a synthesis', *School Organization*, 10(3), 195–202.

——(1995) 'Towards effective school improvement', *School Effectiveness and School Improvement*, 6(3), 265–74.

—— (1996) 'Towards a theory for school improvement', in J. Gray, D. Reynolds and C. Fitz-Gibbon (eds) *Merging Traditions: The Future of Research on School Effectiveness and School Improvement*, London: Cassell.

Hopkins, D., Ainscow, M. and West, M. (1994) *School Improvement in an Era of Change*, London/New York: Cassell.

Hopkins, D., Ainscow, M. and West, M. (in press) 'A case study of the "Improving the Quality of Education for All" school improvement project', in A. Harris (ed.) *Organisational Effectiveness and Improvement in Education*.

Hopkins, D. and Stern, D. (1996) 'Quality teachers, quality schools: international perspectives and policy implications', *Teaching and Teacher Education* (in press).

House, E. R. (1981) 'Three perspectives on innovation: Technological, political and cultural', in R. Lehming and M. Kane (eds), *Improving Schools: Using What We Know*, 17–42. London: Beverley Hills.

Huberman, M. and Miles, M. (1984) *Innovation Up Close*, New York: Plemen.

Joyce, B. (1991) 'The doors to school improvement', *Educational Leadership*, May, 59–62.

—— (1992) 'Cooperative learning and staff development research: teaching the method with the method', *Cooperative Learning*, 12(21), 10–13.

Joyce, B., Hersh, R. and McKibbin, M. (1983) *The Structure of School Improvement*, New York: Longman.

Joyce, B. and Showers, B. (1988) *Student Achievement Through Staff Development*, New York: Longman.

Joyce, B. and Weil, M. (1996) *Models of Teaching (5th Edition)*, Englewood Cliffs, NJ: Prentice-Hall.

Joyce, B., Wolf, J. and Calhoun, E. (1993) *The Self Renewing School*, Alexandria, VA: ASCD.

Kruger, M. (1994) *Sekseverschillen in schoolleiderschap*, Alphen aan de Rijn: Samson H.D. Tjeenk Willink.

Lagerweij, N. A. J. and Haak, E. M. (1994) *Eerst goed kijken . . . de dynamiek van scholen-in-ontwikkeling*, Leuven/Apeldoorn: Garant.

Leithwood, K. (1995) *School Restructuring in British Columbia: Summarizing the Results of a Four-Year Study*. Paper presented at the annual meeting of the American Educational Research Association, San Francisco, April.

Leithwood, K. and Steinback, R. (1995) *Expert Problem Solving*, Albany: State University of New York Press.

Levine, D. and Lezotte, L. (1990) *An Interpretative Review and Analysis of Research and Practice in Unusually Effective Schools*, Madison: University of Winconsin Press.

Louis, K. S. and Kruse, S. D. (1995) *Professionalism and Community*, Thousand Oaks: Corwin Press.

Louis, K. S. and Miles, M. B. (1990) *Improving the Urban High School: What Works and Why*, New York: Teachers' College Press.

McLaughlin, M. (1990) 'The Rand Change Agent Study revisited: Macro perspectives micro realities', *Educational Researcher*, 19(9), 11–16.

Marx, E. C. H. (1975) *De organisatie van scholengemeenschappoen in onderwijskundige optiek*, Groningen: Tjeenk Willink.

Miles, M. (1983) 'Unravelling the mysteries of institutionalisation', *Educational Leadership*, 41(3), 14–19.

—— (1986) 'Research findings on the stages of school improvement', (mimeo), New York: Center for Policy Research.

Mintzberg, H. (1990) *Over veranderen*, (Congresmap). Vlaardingen: Nederlands Studie Centrum.

—— (1992) *Organisatie structuren*, Schoonhoven: Academic Service Economie en Bedrijfskunde.

Murphy, J. and Louis, K. S. (1994) *Reshaping the Principalship Insights From Transformational Reform Efforts*, Thousand Oaks: Corwin Press.

Nisbet, J. (ed.) (1973) *Creativity of the School*, Paris: OECD.

OECD (1989) *Decentralisation and School Improvement*, Paris: OECD–CERI.

Petri, M. (1995) *Samen vliegeren methodiek en resultaten van interactieve school diagnose*, Proefschrift, Leuven: ACCO.

Purkey, S. C. and Smith, M. S. (1983) 'Effective schools – a review', *The Elementary School Journal*, 4, 427–52.

Quinn, R. E. and Rohrbaugh, J. (1983) 'A spatial model of effectiveness criteria: Towards a competing values approach to organizational analysis', *Management Science*, 29(3), 363–77.

Reynolds, D. (1985) *Studying School Effectiveness*, London: Falmer Press.

Rosenholtz, S. J. (1989) *Teachers Workplace: The Social Organization of Schools*, New York/London: Longman.

Rowe, K., Holmes-Smith, P. and Hill, P. (1993) 'The link between school effectiveness research, policy and school improvement'. Paper presented at the 1993 annual conference of the Australian Association for Research in Education, Fremantle, Western Australia, November 22–25.

Rutter, M., Heron, R. and McKibbin, M. (1979) *Fifteen Thousand Hours*, London: Open Books.

Sashkin, M. and Egermeier, J. (1992) *School Change Models and Processes. A review and Synthesis of Research and Practice*, Washington: US Department of Education.

Scheerens, J. (1994) 'The school-level context of instructional effectiveness: A comparison between school effectiveness and restructuring models', *Tijdschrift voor Onderwijsresearch*, 19(1), 26–38.

Sleegers, P. J. C. (1991) *School en beleidsvoering*, Academisch proefschrift, Nijmegen: Universiteitsdrukkerij.
Sleegers, P. J. C., Bergen, Th. C. M. and Giebers, J. H. G. I. (1992) 'School en beleidsvoering', *Pedagogische studien*, 69(3), 177–99.
Stoll, L. and Fink, D. (1996) *Changing Our Schools: Linking School Effectiveness and School Improvement* Buckingham: Open University Press.
Tichy, N. M. (1983) *Managing Strategic Change. Technical, Political and Cultural Dynamics*, New York: Wiley and Sons.
Vandenberghe, R. (1993a) *De determinanten van het professionele handelen van leerkrachten secundair onderwijs en de invloed op de onderwijskwaliteit*, Leuven: Centrum voor Onderwijsbeleid envernieuwing.
——(ed.) (1993b) *Scholen en vernieuwing: een kans tot professionele groei en schoolverbetering*, Leuven: Centrum voor Onderwijsbeleid envernieuwing.
Vandenberghe, R. and Vegt, R. van der (1992) *Scholen in de vernieuwingsarena*, Leuven/Apeldoorn: Garant.
Velzen, W. G. van, (1979) *Autonomy of the School*, S'Hertogenkosch: PKC.
Velzen, W. G. van, Miles, M. B., Ekholm, M., Hameyer, U. and Robin, D. (1985) *Making School Improvement Work*, Leuven/Amersfoort: ACCO.
Voogt, J. C. (1986) 'Werken aan onderwijs verbetering', in A. Reints and J. C. Voogt (eds), *Naar beter onderwijs*, Tilburg: Uitgeverij Zwijsen.
—— (1988) 'Systematic analysis for school improvement (SAS)', in D. Hopkins, *Doing School Based Review*, Leuven: ACCO.
—— (1989) *Scholen doorgelicht; een studie over schooldiagnose*, Academisch proefschrift, De Lier: ABC.
—— (1994) *Instrument voor Schooldiagnose*, Utrecht: APS.
Weiler, H. N. (1990) 'Comparative perspectives on educational decentralization: an exercise in contradiction?', *Educational Evaluation and Policy Analysis*, 12, 443–8.
Wilson, B. C. and Corcoran, T. B. (1988) *Successful Secondary Schools*, London: Falmer Press.
Witziers, B. (1992) *Coordinatie binnen scholen voor voortgezet onderwijs*, Academisch proefschrift, Enschede: z.u.

Chapter 5

Merging school effectiveness and school improvement
The knowledge bases

David Reynolds and Louise Stoll

INTRODUCTION

In Chapters 2, 3 and 4 of this volume we have seen something of the differing orientations that have existed between the two bodies of knowledge historically named 'school effectiveness' and 'school improvement'. Even sometimes in their basic goals concerning what the outcomes of education should be, the two different groups have had different perceptions, as Chapter Two reminded us, although both groups have increasingly converged in their goals and their practices of late, as we have noted in Chapter Four.

This chapter continues to move us forward by considering what the benefits would be of an integrated effectiveness/improvement para-digm in which the goal of creating improved school organisations is deemed sufficiently important to justify a suspension of any historical disciplinary rivalries. In the interests of encouraging further 'synergy' and integration between the perspectives, we outline in this chapter what role effectiveness research and improvement research/practice can perform for the integrated educational enterprise that we wish for, if it were prepared to examine itself and its historic roots critically and if it were prepared to cease 'reactive' posturing and substitute purposive intellectual and practical change.

SCHOOL EFFECTIVENESS AND SCHOOL IMPROVEMENT: AN INTERNATIONAL SURVEY

Whatever one's hopes concerning a 'merged' effectiveness/improve-ment paradigm in the future, it is clear that, historically, there have been problems in the relationship between the two communities. In North America, particularly within the United States, there exists perhaps the closest of the international relationships between school effectiveness and school improvement. At the start of the 1990s, over half of all American school districts were running improvement programmes based upon, or linked to, the effective schools knowledge base (General Accounting Office, 1989; Taylor, 1990), although it must be noted, however, that the knowledge base within the improvement programmes tended to be of the earlier, simplistic variety of 'five factor' theories developed by Edmonds (1979) and popularised by Lezotte (1989), rather than the one more recently developed from a considerably more advanced research base by researchers like Stringfield and Teddlie (Teddlie and Stringfield, 1993). In addition, there have been in the United States the well known demonstration projects which have involved the direct, controlled transfer of effectiveness knowledge into school improvement programmes, which have demonstrated enhanced school effectiveness (e.g. McCormack-Larkin, 1985). In Canada likewise, there have been programmes which involve the utilisation of school effectiveness knowledge within school improvement programmes (Stoll and Fink, 1992, 1994), and the school effectiveness knowledge base has also penetrated many other ongoing improvement projects (see reviews in Sackney, 1985, 1989).

In spite of this evident relationship between the two bodies of knowledge at the level of practice, at the intellectual level there is much less of a relationship or commonality of perspective between the scholars who have contributed to their respective knowledge bases. In part, this may be because school improvement scholars have reacted against the simplistic nature of past North American school effectiveness literature. Whatever the precise reasons, school improvement scholars such as Fullan, Hall and Miles rarely base their school improvement strategies upon the knowledge of school effectiveness researchers. Fullan (1991), for example, refers to only half a dozen school effectiveness studies from the United States, only two from the United Kingdom and none from any of the other societies like Australia, the Netherlands or New Zealand in which major school effectiveness projects have been carried out. Were we to take Fullan and the other improvement writers noted above, a survey of their bibliographies would suggest that only about 2 or 3 per cent of their total references are from writers commonly regarded as writing within the school effectiveness research paradigm. Were we also to take the American school effectiveness research community and look at the nature of their references, probably only about 1 per cent of total references would relate to writers conventionally located within the paradigm of school improvement.

The situation of two separate, discrete bodies of knowledge and two separate research communities that exist in North America is in evidence in most other parts of the world; indeed, in certain parts of the world; the separation is even more in evidence. In the United Kingdom, there was, until recently, little collaboration between those working within the school effectiveness and school improvement paradigms, little practitioner take-up of the knowledge base of school effectiveness (Mortimore, 1991; Reynolds, 1991), little use of the research in school improvement or school development programmes (Reid *et al.*, 1987), and little appreciation or referencing of school effectiveness material in the works of 'school improvers' (and vice versa). Indeed the British Economic and Social Research Council funded, in 1993, a programme of symposia and seminars for persons in the two fields of effectiveness and improvement, explicitly to make possible the forming of links (Gray *et al.*, 1996).

In other parts of the world the situation is similar to that in Britain. New Zealand, for example, was the site of pioneering school effectiveness research (Ramsay *et al.*, 1982), but there are no current signs of engagement with this knowledge base by those working within the 'school improvement through decentralisation' paradigm that has existed since the Picot Report in the late 1980s. The Netherlands now has perhaps the world's most extensive empirical, quantitative research base within the field of school effectiveness (see Creemers and Scheerens, 1989), but there is little evidence of school effectiveness based school improvement programmes, nor of any penetration of school effectiveness research knowledge into schools through the development planning which is now mandatory within Dutch schools. Australia, too, has a small school effectiveness research base (see Chapman and Stevens, 1989), and indeed some of this knowledge has been linked to school improvement through the school self management approach of Caldwell and Spinks (1988). But again, more developmentally-oriented material from Australia shows only limited take up of, or reliance on, school effectiveness literature. Indeed, the Australian school improvement tradition relates primarily to the literature on educational management and administration, itself notable for the absence of linkages with the school effectiveness research base and for the presence of overt hostility towards school effectiveness persons. Only in Israel internationally do we see any systematic application of school effectiveness findings in school improvement programmes (Bashi, 1995).

It will be clear from this, and from earlier chapters of this volume, that underlying these two distinctive bodies of scholarship, and the separation of the two groups of scholars, have been two very distinctive intellectual traditions and histories. In the following two sections of this chapter we examine more closely the values, research and practice implicit in both approaches.

THE SCHOOL IMPROVEMENT PARADIGM

Approaches to school improvement have, over the past thirty years, been characterised by two very different sets of assumptions, as outlined in Chapter Four and codified in Table 5.1.

In the 1960s and 1970s, school improvement in the United States, the United Kingdom and internationally, displayed a number of paradigmatic characteristics. It was linked as an enterprise to a technological view of school improvement, in which mostly curriculum innovations were brought to schools from outside, and then introduced 'top down'. The innovations were based upon knowledge produced by persons outside the school, the focus was on the school's formal organisation and curriculum, the outcomes were taken as given, and the innovation was targeted at the school more than the individual practitioner. The whole improvement edifice was based upon a positivistic, quantitative evaluation of effects. The worldwide failure of this model of school improvement to generate more than partial take-up by schools of the curricula or organisational innovations became an established finding within the educational discourse

Table 5.1 The characteristics of two school improvement paradigms

	1960s	1980s
Orientation	'top-down'	'bottom-up'
Knowledge base	elite knowledge	practitioner knowledge
Target	organisation or curriculum based	process based
Outcomes	pupil outcome oriented	school process oriented
Goals	outcomes as given	outcomes problematic
Focus	school	teacher
Methodology of evaluation	quantitative	qualitative
Site	outside school	within school
Focus	part of school	whole school

of the 1970s, explained widely – as we noted in Chapter 4 – as due to a lack of teacher 'ownership'.

Out of the recognition of this failure came the new improvement paradigm of the early 1980s, which is still reflected in much of the writing on school improvement that is current today and which indeed is reflected in much of the conceptualisation in Chapter 4. This new orientation celebrated a 'bottom up' approach to school improvement, in which the improvement attempts were 'owned' by those at the school level, although outside school consultants or experts could put their knowledge forward for possible utilisation. This new approach tended to celebrate the 'folklore' or practical knowledge of practitioners rather than the knowledge base of researchers, and focused upon needed changes to educational processes, rather than to school management, or to organisational features which were regarded as reified constructs. It wanted the outcomes or goals of school improvement programmes to be debated and discussed, rather than merely accepted as given. Those working within this paradigm also tended to operate at the level of the practitioner as well as at the level of the school, with a qualitative and naturalistically orientated evaluation of the enterprise being preferred to quantitative measurement. The improvement attempt was 'whole school' oriented and school based, rather than outside school or course based (see Reynolds, 1988).

There is little doubt that the new school improvement paradigm outlined above was deficient in terms of actually generating school improvement, as some of its proponents began to realise. The process oriented 'journey' of school improvement was still stressed, but by the late 1980s the journey was also undertaken in order to enable schools to evaluate their processes and outcomes. This attitude was exemplified in the work of the OECD-sponsored International School Improvement Project (ISIP), and the knowledge that emanated from it that has been frequently referred to already in this book.

THE SCHOOL EFFECTIVENESS PARADIGM

The school effectiveness research paradigm has, of course, a very different intellectual history and has exhibited a very different set of core beliefs concerning operationalisation, conceptualisation and measurement by comparison with the changing approaches of the school improvers, as will already have been clear from Chapters 2 and 3. It has been strongly committed to the use of quantitative methods, since many researchers were concerned to refute the 'schools make no difference' hypothesis advanced by Coleman *et al.* (1966) and Jencks *et al.* (1972), by utilising the same conventional methods of empirical research as their perceived opponents had utilised. Many effectiveness researchers have also believed that teachers, especially North American ones, would pay more attention to work conducted within the quantitative paradigm than that from a more naturalistic perspective.

School effectiveness researchers have also been primarily concerned with student academic outcomes, which is not surprising given the political history of school effectiveness research in the United States, where it has grown and built on the beliefs of Ron Edmonds and his associates that 'all children can learn'. Processes within schools only have an importance within the school effectiveness paradigm to the extent that they affect outcomes – indeed, one 'back maps' within the paradigm from outcomes to processes. The school effectiveness paradigm furthermore regards student and school outcomes as fundamentally unproblematic, and as givens. Indeed, in much of the North American effectiveness research, only a limited range of outcomes is used, reflecting the acceptance of 'official' educational definitions of the school as an academic institution. School effectiveness researchers, indeed, often talk of a 'good' or 'excellent' school as if that were unproblematic.

The school effectiveness paradigm is also organisationally based rather than process based in terms of its analytic and descriptive orientation, preferring to restrict itself to the more easily quantifiable or measurable. As an example, Fullan's (1985) process factors, such as 'a feel for the process of leadership', 'a guiding value system', or 'intense interaction and communication', are largely eschewed in favour of a concentration upon organisationally and behaviourally oriented process variables such as 'clear goals and high expectations' and/or 'parental involvement and support'. Additionally, the focus within the school improvement paradigm on the attitudinal, and on the culture of schools, is replaced within school effectiveness research by a focus on the more easily measured behaviour of persons.

A last couple of differences are also clear. School effectiveness research has customarily celebrated the importance of a very limited range of outcomes, mostly academic and mostly concerned with the acquisition of basic skills. Indeed, all the early American work focused upon academic achievement virtually exclusively (see review in Reynolds *et al.*, 1994). School improvement research in the 1980s, by contrast, often conceptualised outcomes more broadly. Often, in the British tradition, the aim of the improvement attempt or project was to debate the 'possible' goals of education, as against the limited 'official' goals, as part of the process of securing professional development and school improvement. In most accounts of their processes (e.g. Hopkins, 1987), it seems that multiple goals formed the intellectual base of school improvement historically.

Finally, school effectiveness has differed from school improvement in that it has been concerned to celebrate the 'end state' by describing what it is that schools which are effective are actually 'like', whereas school improvement has been more concerned to discover what it is that has been done to bring schools to that state. The orientation of school effectiveness has been a 'static' one, concerned with the 'steady state' of effectiveness; the orientation of school improvement has been a 'dynamic' one, focusing upon 'change over time'.

THE BEGINNINGS OF MERGER

From the outline of the history of the two paradigms in the previous sections, and from our earlier chapters, it can be seen that the disciplines of school effectiveness and school improvement are 'coming from' very different places intellectually, methodologically and theoretically. A crude characterisation that contrasts both approaches is given in Table 5.2.

There is recent evidence, as we have noted before in this volume, that some of those who are appreciative of aspects of the school improvement tradition have realised the necessity for 'paradigmatic change' within that paradigm, and a changed approach to school improvement is becoming increasingly common. The Department of Education and Science project on *School Development Plans* (SDPs) in England and Wales, for example, was an attempt to develop a strategy that would, among other things, help governors, heads and teachers to take control of the process of change (see Hargreaves *et al.*, 1989; Hargreaves & Hopkins, 1991). The work of Bruce Joyce and his colleagues (see Joyce *et al.*, 1983, 1992; Joyce and Showers, 1988) has also for some time transcended both paradigms. Although located within the school improvement tradition, Joyce argues strongly for the raising of student achievement through the utilisation of specific models of teaching and staff development designs.

An increasing number of scholars within the school effectiveness community have also begun to argue for the interpenetration and

Table 5.2 The separate traditions of school effectiveness and school improvement

School effectiveness	School improvement in the 1980s
Focus on schools	Focus on individual teachers or groups of teachers
Focus on school organisation	Focus on school processes
Data driven, with emphasis on outcomes	Rare empirical evaluation of effects of changes
Quantitative in orientation	Qualitative in orientation
Lack of knowledge about how to implement change strategies	Concerned with change in schools exclusively
More concerned with change in pupil outcomes	More concerned with journey of school improvement than its destination
More concerned with schools at a point in time	More concerned with schools as changing
Based on research knowledge	Focus on practitioner knowledge
Limited range of outcomes	Concern with multiple outcomes
Concerned with schools that are effective	Concern with how schools *become* effective
Static orientation (school as it is)	Dynamic orientation (school as it has been or might be)

synthesis of both bodies of knowledge in the interests of improving pupil performance and school quality. Mortimore (1991: 223) has argued for transferring 'the energy, knowledge and skills of school effectiveness research to the study of school improvement'. Stoll and Fink (1992: 104) maintain that 'it is only when school effectiveness research is merged with what is known about school improvement, planned change and staff development, that schools and teachers can be empowered and supported in their growth towards effectiveness'. Murphy (1992), himself a school effectiveness researcher who, in his own empirical work, has existed within the effectiveness paradigm outlined earlier, now also wants to move in directions that celebrate the potential not just of conventional school improvement programmes, but of a more radical 'restructuring' of the educational system, its power relations, and the teaching–learning process in schools. The mission statement of the journal *School Effectiveness and School Improvement* (Creemers and Reynolds, 1990) also argued for the still, small voice of empirical rationality being utilised jointly to assess the validity both of existing models of school improvement and of our existing, simplistic, factor-based theories of school effectiveness.

THE NEEDS FOR MERGER

The potential benefits of a merged or integrated approach to improving school quality become even clearer if one considers how central the two disciplines or 'paradigms' are to each other. To take the practice of school improvement first, it is clear that knowledge is needed concerning the factors within schools and classrooms that should be changed to enhance processes and outcomes. Effectiveness research can provide that knowledge. Likewise, school improvement and its consequent changes to school and classroom factors can provide a testing ground for school effectiveness theories that relate processes and outcomes, and can therefore show if there are causal links involved.

What the two paradigms can contribute to each other and to enhanced educational quality is minimised because of a consistent lack of synchronisation between the effectiveness and improvement enterprises and the needs of the educational system and its practitioners for high quality knowledge that will improve practice. To take the *deficiencies in existing school effectiveness* first:

- There are very few studies at the level of 'case studies' of effective, or even more so ineffective, schools that would show the interrelationships between school process variables and could paint a picture for improvement practitioners of the fine-grained reality of school and classroom processes. The American study by Rosenholtz (1989), and some of the recent 'mixed methodology' work from the 'Louisiana School Effectiveness Study' of Stringfield and Teddlie (1990), are exceptions to this trend internationally, but even they do not get particularly 'close to the action'. In the UK, for example, we still have no in-depth, qualitative portrait of the effective school equivalent to Louis and Miles's (1990) *Improving the Urban High School*, which provides excellent case studies of process variables, although the National Commission on Education's (1995) examination of eleven schools which were successful 'against the odds' has encouraged a start in this area. The absence of rich case study explanations reduces the practitioner relevance of the effectiveness research and makes the transfer of knowledge to improvement programmes difficult.
- School effectiveness studies are very deficient at the level of the study of 'processes' rather than factors, since effectiveness researchers have considerably more experience at the level of school organisational factors. School processes defined in terms of atti-

tudes, values, relationships and climate have been somewhat neglected, therefore, even though school improvement needs information on these factors within schools, given their centrality to the process of improvement and development that we have already seen in Chapter 4.

- School effectiveness studies customarily show a 'snapshot' of a school at a point in time, not an evolutionary and moving picture of a school over time, a neglect which hinders the usefulness of the knowledge for purposes of school development. School improvement necessitates ideas about how schools came to be effective (or for that matter ineffective), in order to replicate (or for that matter eradicate) the processes. This necessitates a dynamic, evolutionary, evolving and 'change over time' orientation within school effectiveness research.

- School effectiveness studies, with the exception of work by Rosenholtz (1989) and Coleman and Laroque (1991), have tended to neglect the importance and potential impact of other educational institutions, arrangements and layers above the level of the school. As Hopkins (1990: 188) notes when discussing school improvement conducted within the ISIP 'much thought . . . was given to the way in which improvement policies are established at various levels . . . to the structured factors related to support, e.g. external support. . . . Much of the effective schools literature appears to take such "meso level" issues as unproblematic, yet the ISIP case studies suggest that this is just not so.' School improvement needs to be informed by knowledge as to what conditions outside the level of the school are necessary to generate process and outcome improvement, although recent work by Stoll and Fink (1994, 1996) does begin to explore this issue.

- School effectiveness research, whether of North American, British or Dutch origin, tends towards the generation of lists of organisational factors within schools that are associated with pupil outcomes, yet, of course, what school improvement needs is not the knowledge of which ten, twenty or thirty factors may be useful enhancers of outcomes if changed, but which one or two key factors should be changed first. The need for change strategies that relate to a small and discrete number of factors is magnified by the need to alter those variables within schools which are the key determinants of other process variables. No school effectiveness study so far has attempted to isolate the direction and strength of the influences that link school process variables together, which means that the phasing of improvement programmes that is essential to stop overload is very difficult in practice.

- School effectiveness research, to compound the difficulties already noted, cannot even prove conclusively which process variables are causes of school effectiveness and which are effects. If we take as an example the well established link between teachers' high academic expectations of their pupils and their students' good results in examinations or tests of attainment, it may be that the direction of the relationship is a positive one, or that academic success may, by contrast, generate high expectations, since the experience of high examination passes at school level may lead to an expectation of them continuing. Alternatively, there may be interactive influences. The directionality of the relationship – crucial for the decision concerning what to target for improvement – is not established from the research base for this variable and for many other variables within the school effectiveness knowledge base.

- School effectiveness knowledge also misses the chance of satisfaction of the needs of school improvement by being dated. Improvement schemes in the 1990s need to be based on knowledge that is generated from schools that reflect the characteristics of schools in the 1990s, not the schools of the 1970s and 1980s. At the level of what makes for effective schooling, process factors such as the assertive principal instructional leadership which was associated with school effectiveness in the 1980s may not be associated in the same way in the 1990s, when demands for ownership by teachers may have changed the educational cultural context. Outcomes appropriate for measurement in the 1980s, such as academic achievement or examination attainment, may not be the only outcomes appropriate to the 1990s, where new goals concerning knowledge of 'how to learn' or ability in mastering information technology may be necessary.

- School effectiveness research has rarely been 'fine grained' enough to provide information that is needed for school improvement, since the variation in 'what works' by contexts has been a focus only of a very limited amount of recent North American work (Hallinger and Murphy, 1986; Wimpelberg et al., 1989). School improvement needs more than the notion of what works across context in the average school, and needs more than data on the relationships between school processes and outcomes for all schools. It needs knowledge of the factors that will generate improvement in particular schools in particular socio-economic and cultural contexts. Since only a small amount of our school effectiveness data base is analysed by context, the delineation of the precise variables that school improvement needs to target to affect outcomes is clearly impossible at present. The needed disaggregation of samples of schools to permit the analysis of contextual variation needs, of course, also to focus on the precise organisational and process variables that may be responsible for the differential effectiveness of schools with different groups of pupils within them (Nuttall *et al.*, 1989), or pupils taking different subjects (Sammons *et al.*, 1995). Findings of differential school effects also necessitate investigations oriented towards differentiated analyses of within-school factors, rather than the present concentration upon 'common' school process factors.

• Many persons wishing to improve schools often find themselves working in historically ineffective educational settings, yet the knowledge base within school effectiveness may not be necessarily easily applicable to those settings. It is probable that the ineffective school may possess variables at the level of interpersonal problems, projections, defences and the like which do not exist in the effective school. Yet the possible existence of these 'ghosts' or 'shadows' on the change process seem to be rarely considered by researchers. The knowledge required by improvers of ineffective schools is simply not found in school effectiveness research, where the good practice of effective schools is simply 'back mapped' on to ineffective schools, and then assumed to be sufficient to make them improve.

Moving on from what changed school effectiveness research could give to school improvement programmes, it is clear that a somewhat changed school improvement enterprise could also perform the valuable function of contributing to our knowledge about the validity of effectiveness factors as well as potentially improving school practice.

At the moment, *school improvement research and practice is too deficient in the following ways* to enable it to fulfil its promise:

• School improvement practice/research only rarely measures the impact of changes in improvement programmes upon the outcomes of pupils or students. Part of the explanation for this may be the historical tendency of school improvement to celebrate certain styles of professional practice, because of its association with the training needs and desires of the teaching profession within schools. Another part of the explanation may be the reluctance of many within the school improvement paradigm to be explicit about what the nature of school outcomes, or the educational goals of their programmes, really are. However, the absence of data on improvement programme effects restricts the ability of those within the school effectiveness tradition to help knowledge expand, in terms of further understanding the possible causal relationships between school processes and school outcomes.

- Those engaged in school improvement need urgently to pay attention to the implications of multi-level modelling procedures for their programmes. As noted earlier, the evidence from effectiveness research that schools can have differential effects upon their pupils (Nuttall *et al.*, 1989), and that schools effective for some groups of pupils may actually be less effective for others, has wide-ranging implication for school improvement. These results imply that improvement attempts need urgently to move away from the much vaunted 'whole-school' strategies towards more finely targeted programmes that may vary within the school in terms of their content, their focus and their target group. Above all, schools need to examine assessment data, whether these are academic results, attendance patterns, attitudes or any other measures of students' progress and development, and look for variations between different subsets of the population. By taking these differences into account, and by focusing improvement at the level of boys/girls, high ability/low ability pupils, and pupils from ethnic minorities/pupils from 'host' cultures, it would be possible to generate more appropriate school change strategies. This would in turn allow researchers to generate evidence about differentially effective school processes, as the effects of the change attempts were targeted within schools.
- Besides focusing more on outcomes, school improvement researchers also need to 'polish their independent variables'. Knowing that student achievement has increased is not much use for policy making, if we do not know why the change has occurred. Although this point is linked to the three previous ones, it specifically demands more theoretical precision from school improvers in clarifying the links in the school improvement chain, their anticipated impact and in developing ways of measuring them.
- School improvement research needs to refocus its activities, from placing a greater emphasis on the school level to highlighting the level of the classroom. A considerable volume of research now

exists which suggests that teachers' focal concerns are with the content of their curricula and the nature of their instructional practice, rather than with the wider organisation of the school. Yet many school improvement efforts have, until recently, neglected the primacy of instruction. By not focusing on instruction, school improvement runs the risk of manipulating variables only at the level of the school, which, in most recent research, explains much less of the variation in student outcomes than do variables at the instructional or classroom level (see, for a review, Creemers, 1992).

- School improvement needs to move beyond its current status as what West and Hopkins (1995) have called 'a glorified staff development activity'. Many of the growing number of networks or school improvement 'clubs' reviewed by Myers and Stoll (1993) and Stoll and Mortimore (1995) involve, when looked at closely, a traditional alliance of local authority professional developers, University Departments of Education that customarily have a strong stake in continuing professional development activities, and the senior personnel in schools. The three groups might be seen as celebrating each other's importance and status, if evaluation of the gain educational 'consumers', children or their parents, obtain from their activities is not addressed.

- A sixth area of concern is that school improvement has customarily adopted a 'rational technical' or 'rational empirical' approach which may be inappropriate to a real school community. There are more and more hints within the literature that some schools may be 'non-rational', in that they harbour delusions and associated cultures that may be an understandable reaction to their problems (Reynolds, 1996). Ineffective schools may, for example, blame their children for their poor levels of educational 'value added', or may additionally have an emotional commitment to certain ways of working that are not productive. More generally, as West and Hopkins (1995) point out, many schools may not have the structures, the experience or the strategies to move the school, because of the existence of the 'ghosts' of past practice, or the 'shadows' of present tensions.

- School improvement may need to consider the prominence it has given to the 'voice' of the teacher. This is understandable, given that using the perceptions and language of teachers helps bring to life for teachers the improvement process, in ways that use of research perspective or language may not. As West and Hopkins (1995) note, however, 'It is all well and good to start with the reality of teachers but it is a travesty when one ends there as well. It is . . . all too easy to move beyond critical collaboration into the pooling of rationalisations.'

CONCLUSIONS

In this chapter we have seen that there are historic differences and tensions between school effectiveness research and school improvement research, and practice differences that have affected virtually every part of their intellectual structure on 'paradigms'. In methodological preference (quantitative or qualitative), in orientation (process change or outcome concern), in knowledge base (professional researcher or practitioner) and in focus (school as static, or school as changing), the two groups have not related professionally because they have not related intellectually.

We have also noted a number of persons who believe that the separation of the two knowledge bases is practically unhealthy for schools and intellectually damaging for both of the groups of researchers in the two areas, since potentially useful insights are not utilised within the two paradigms because they come from the much maligned 'other' group. We have concluded that there has been a vast historic mismatch between what school effectiveness research has done and the precise needs of those who, in practice or research, are concerned with school improvement, and between what school improvement has done and the knowledge needs of school effectiveness.

We now move on in Chapter 6 to outline those projects and paradigms that are beginning to emerge that are not 'either' effectiveness 'or' improvement in their intellectual ancestry, but represent problem centred 'blends' of the two formerly separate bodies of knowledge and insights.

REFERENCES

Bashi, J. (1995) 'Key national assignments for advancing and improving the Israeli education system during the 1990's', in B. P. M. Creemers and N. Osinga (eds), *ICSEI Country Reports*, Leeuwarden: GCO.

Caldwell, B. and Spinks, J. (1988) *The Self Managing School*, Lewes: Falmer Press.

Chapman, J. and Stevens, S. (1989) 'Australia', in D. Reynolds, B. P. M. Creemers and T. Peters (eds), *School Effectiveness and Improvement*, Groningen: RION.

Coleman, J. S., Campbell, E., Hobson, C., McPartland, J., Mood, A., Weinfeld, F. and York, R. (1966) *Equality of Educational Opportunity*, Washington, DC: National Center for Educational Statistics.

Coleman, P. and Laroque, L. (1991) *Struggling to be Good Enough*, Lewes: Falmer Press.

Creemers, B. (1992) 'School effectiveness and effective instruction – the need for a further relationship', in J. Bashi and Z. Sass, *School Effectiveness and Improvement*, Jerusalem: Hebrew University Press.

Creemers, B. and Reynolds, D. (1990) 'School effectiveness and school improvement – a mission statement', *School Effectiveness and School Improvement*, 1(1), 1–3.

Creemers, B. and Scheerens, J. (eds) (1989) 'Developments in school effectiveness research', a special issue of *International Journal of Educational Research*, 13(7), 685–825.

Edmonds, R. R. (1979) 'Effective schools for the urban poor', *Educational Leadership*, 37(15–18), 20–4.

Fullan, M. (1985) 'Change processes and strategies at the local level', *Elementary School Journal*, 85(13), 391–421.

—— (1991) *The New Meaning of Educational Change*, London: Cassell; New York: Teachers' College Press.

—— (1992) 'Visions that blind', *Educational Leadership*, 49(5), 19–20.

General Accounting Office (1989) *Effective Schools Programmes – Their Extent and Characteristics*, Gaithersberg, MD: General Accounting Office.

Gray, J., Reynolds, D., Fitz-Gibbon, C. and Jesson, D. (1996) *Merging Traditions: The Future of Research on School Effectiveness and Improvement*, London: Cassell.

Hallinger, P. and Murphy, J. (1986) 'The social context of effective schools', *American Journal of Education*, 94, 328–55.

Hargreaves, D. H. and Hopkins, D. (1991) *The Empowered School: The Management and Practice of Development Planning*, London: Cassell.

Hargreaves, D. H., Hopkins, D., Leask, M., Connolly, J. and Robinson, P. (1989) *Planning for School Development: Advice to Governors, Headteachers and Teachers*, London: Department of Education and Science.

Holly, P. (1990) 'Catching the wave of the future: moving beyond school effectiveness by redesigning schools', *School Organisation*, 10(3), 195–212.

Hopkins, D. (1987) *Improving the Quality of Schooling*, Lewes: Falmer Press.

—— (1990) 'The International School Improvement Project (ISIP) and effective schooling: towards a synthesis', *School Organisation*, 10(3), 129–94.

—— (1991) 'Changing school culture through development planning', in S. Riddell and S. Brown (eds), *School Effectiveness Research: Messages for School Improvement*, Edinburgh: HMSO.

Hopkins, D., Ainscow, M. and West, M. (1994) *School Improvement in an Era of Change*, London: Cassell.

Jencks, C. S., Smith, M., Ackland, H., Bane, M. J., Cohen, D., Gintis, H., Heyns, B. and Micholson, S. (1972) *Inequality: A Reassessment of the Effect of Family and Schooling in America*, New York: Basic Books.

Joyce, B. and Showers, B. (1988) *Student Achievement Through Staff Development*, New York: Longman.

Joyce, B., Hersh, R. and McKibbin, M. (1983) *The Structure of School Improvement*, New York: Longman.

Joyce, B., Showers, B. and Weil, M. (1992) *Models of Teaching* (4th Edition), Englewood Cliffs, NJ: Prentice-Hall.

Lezotte, L. (1989) 'School improvement based on the effective schools research', *International Journal of Educational Research*, 13(7), 815–25.

Louis, K. S. and Miles, M. B. (1990) *Improving the Urban High School: What Works and Why*, New York: Teachers' College Press; London: Cassell.

McCormack-Larkin, M. (1985) 'Ingredients of a successful school effectiveness project', *Educational Leadership*, March, 31–7.

Maughan, B., Ouston, J., Pickles, A. and Rutter, M. (1990) 'Can schools change 1 – Outcomes at six London secondary schools', *School Effectiveness and Improvement*, 1(3), 188–210.

Mortimore, P. (1991) 'School effectiveness research: which way at the crossroads?, *School Effectiveness and School Improvement*, 2(3), 213–29.

Mortimore, P., Sammons, P., Stoll, L., Lewis, D. and Ecob, R. (1988) *School Matters: The Junior Years*, Salisbury: Open Books; Berkeley: University of California Press.

Murphy, J. (1992) 'School effectiveness and school restructuring: Contributions to educational improvement', *School Effectiveness and School Improvement*, 3(2), 90–109.

Myers, K. and Stoll, L. (1993) 'Mapping the movement', *Education*, 182(3), 51.

National Commission on Education (1995) *Success Against the Odds*, London: Routledge.

Nuttall, D., Goldstein, H., Prosser, R. and Rasbash, H. (1989). 'Differential school effectiveness', *International Journal of Educational Research*, 13(7), 769–76.

Ramsay, P. D. K., Sneddon, D. G., Grenfell, J. and Ford, I. (1982) 'Successful vs unsuccessful schools: a South Auckland study', *Australia and New Zealand Journal of Sociology*, 19(1), 272–314.

Reid, K., Hopkins, D. and Holly, P. (1987). *Towards The Effective School*, Oxford: Blackwell.

Reynolds, D. (1988) 'British school improvement research: the contribution of qualitative studies', *International Journal of Qualitative Studies in Education*, 1(2), 143–54.

—— (1991) 'school effectiveness in secondary schools', in S. Riddell and S. Brown (eds), *School Effectiveness Research: Messages for School Improvement*, Edinburgh: HMSO.

—— (1992) 'School effectiveness and school improvement in the 1990s', in D. Reynolds and P. Cuttance (eds), *School Effectiveness*, London: Cassell.

—— (1996) 'Turning around ineffective schools: Some evidence and some speculations', in J. Gray, D. Reynolds, C. Fitz-Gibbon and D. Jesson (eds), *Merging Traditions: The Future of Research on School Effectiveness and School Improvement*, London: Cassell.

Reynolds, D., Creemers, B. P. M., Nesselrodt, P. S., Schaffer, E. C., Stringfield,

S. and Teddlie, C. (1994) *Advances in School Effectiveness Research and Practice*, Oxford: Elsevier Science.

Reynolds, D., Davie, R. and Phillips, D. (1989). 'The Cardiff programme – an effective school improvement programme based on school effectiveness research', in B. P. M. Creemers and J. Scheerens (eds), 'Developments in school effectiveness research', a special issue of *International Journal of Educational Research*, 13(7), 800–14.

Reynolds, D., Sullivan, M and Murgatroyd, S. J. (1987) *The Comprehensive Experiment*, Lewes: Falmer Press.

Rosenholtz, S. (1989) *Teachers' Workplace: The Social Organization of Schools,* New York: Longman.

Rutter, M., Maughan, B., Mortimore, P. and Ouston, J. (1979) *Fifteen Thousand Hours: Secondary Schools and Their Effects on Children*, London: Open Books; Boston: Harvard University Press.

Sackney, L. (1985) 'School district imperatives for effective schools', *The Canadian School Executive*, 16(2), 2–13.

—— (1989) 'School effectiveness and improvement: the Canadian scene', in D. Reynolds, B. Creemers and T. Peters (eds), *School Effectiveness and Improvement*, Groningen: RION.

Sammons, P., Thomas, S., Mortimore, P., Cairns, R., Bausor, J., Walker, A. (1995) *Understanding School and Departmental Differences in Academic Effectiveness: findings from case studies of selected outlier secondary schools in Inner London*. Paper presented to the International Congress for School Effectiveness and Improvement, Leeuwarden.

Schmuck, R. R. and Miles, M. (eds) (1971) *Organization Development in Schools*, Palo Alto, CA: National Press Books.

Sirotnik, K. A. (1987) *The School as the Centre of Change*, (Occasional Paper No.5), Seattle WA: Center for Educational Renewal.

Stoll, L. (1992) 'Teacher growth in the effective school', in M. Fullan and H. Hargreaves (eds), *Teacher Development and Educational Change*, London: Falmer Press.

Stoll, L. and Fink, D. (1989) 'An effective schools project: the Halton Approach', in D. Reynolds, B. Creemers and T. Peters (eds), *School Effectiveness and Improvement*, Groningen: RION.

—— (1992) 'Effecting school change: the Halton approach', *School Effectiveness and School Improvement*, 3(1), 19–41.

—— (1994) 'School effectiveness and school improvement: voices from the field', *School Effectiveness and School Improvement*, 5(2), 149–77.

—— (1996) *Changing Our Schools: Linking School Effectiveness and School Improvement*, Buckingham: Open University Press.

Stoll, L. and Mortimore, P. (1995) *School Effectiveness and School Improvement*, Viewpoint Number 2, London: University of London Institute of Education.

Stringfield, S. and Teddlie, C. (1990) 'School improvement effects: qualitative and quantitative data from four naturally occurring experiments in Phases 3 and 4 of the Louisiana School Effectiveness Study', *School Effectiveness and School Improvement*, 1(2), 139–61.

Taylor, B. O. (ed.) (1990) *Case Studies in Effective Schools Research*, Madison, Wisconsin: National Center for Effective Schools.

Teddlie, C. and Stringfield, S. (1993) *Schools Do Make A Difference*, New York: Teachers' College Press.

Velzen, W. van, Miles, M., Eckholm, M., Hameyer, U. and Robin, D. (1985) *Making School Improvement Work*, Leuven: ACCO.

West, M. D. and Hopkins, D. (1995) 'Re-emphasising school effectiveness and school improvement'. Paper presented to the European Educational Research Association, Bath.

Wimpelberg, R., Teddlie, C. and Stringfield, S. (1989) 'Sensitivity to context: the past and future of effective schools research', *Educational Administration Quarterly*, 25, 82–107.

Chapter 6

Merging school effectiveness and school improvement
Practical examples

Louise Stoll, David Reynolds, Bert Creemers and David Hopkins

INTRODUCTION

We noted in the previous chapter the two groups of persons who have been involved in attempting to improve the quality of education. School effectiveness researchers have examined schooling in order to find out why some schools are more effective than others in promoting positive outcomes (see review by Sammons *et al.*, 1995), and what characteristics are most commonly found in schools that are effective for their pupils (Reynolds *et al.*, 1989; Cotton, 1995; Sammons *et al.*, 1995). School improvement researchers have focused their studies on the processes that schools go through to become more successful and sustain this improvement (Miles and Ekholm, 1985; van Velzen, 1987; Louis and Miles, 1990; Fullan, 1991).

In the latter years of the 1980s and the early years of the 1990s, however, there have emerged in a number of countries intervention projects which are *neither* effectiveness based *nor* school improvement oriented, as defined by the limits of the old disciplines conceptualised and outlined in Chapters 2, 3, 4 and 5. Much of this 'convergence' or 'synergy' between the two paradigms has, in fact, resulted from practitioners and local authority/district policymakers borrowing from both traditions because they do not share the ideological commitment to one or the other way of working of researchers in the fields; while some has arisen through the effects of the International Congress for School Effectiveness and Improvement in breaking down disciplinary as well geographical boundaries.

Sometimes the adoption of ideas from research has been somewhat uncritical; for example, the numerous attempts to apply findings from one specific context to another, entirely different, context when research has increasingly demonstrated significant contextual differences (Hallinger and Murphy, 1985; Teddlie *et al.*, 1989). Sometimes it is clear that projects are partial in their adoption of material from both paradigms – some projects reflect on an understanding of what makes schools effective but do so in the absence of an 'action plan' about how to get to the destination, while other projects have celebrated the 'core' school improvement ideas of ownership, collegiality and laterality without much acknowledgement of the key areas of school process and organisation on which to focus their attention.

Nevertheless, there are a number of projects in action that represent no less than a 'new wave' of thinking about how we improve school quality. A number are now outlined but, before outlining them in detail, it is important to note their general characteristics by comparison with the traditional type of school improvement programmes that we described as characterising the 1980s in Chapter Four. In these novel programmes:

• Pupil outcomes in academic (and often social) areas are regarded as the key 'success criteria', rather than the measures to do with teacher perception of the innovations which had been used historically.
• These outcomes are increasingly assessed by use of 'hard' quantitative data, that is regarded as necessary to build commitment and confidence among those taking part and to measure the success or failure of the project initiative.
• Bodies of knowledge from school effectiveness, school improvement and school development are used to resource programmes, with a problem-centred orientation being used in which philosophical judgements about the nature of appropriate strategies is suspended in favour of a 'what works' approach that is distinctly non-denominational.
• The learning level, the instructional behaviour of teachers and the classroom level, are increasingly being targeted for explicit programme attention as well as the school level – a marked contrast, again, with work from the 1980s where 'the school' was often the sole focus. The ISIP study itself had reflected this focus, as we noted above in Chapter 4.

It is easy to understand why the 'lever' of the school level had been pulled so frequently, since, of course, school improvement persons and school effectiveness persons have had close relationships with senior school level personnel. Senior school level personnel have gone on the courses run by school effectiveness and school improvement persons. The policy discourse in most societies has concerned the school level, not the classroom level. In some societies such as the United Kingdom, there is indeed no recent knowledge base or literature about teacher effectiveness or on practices at classroom level which can potentiate student achievement which would lead to a balance with the past obsession with the school level.

It is clear, though, that the neglect of coherent focus upon classrooms has been very costly indeed. First, it is clear that the greatest variation is within schools by department and by individual, rather than between schools. Put simply, the classroom learning level has maybe two or three times the influence on student achievement than the school level does (Creemers, 1994).

Additionally, the reluctance to focus upon classrooms directly, or to turn round interventions at school level 'downwards' in schools until they impact on classrooms, has hindered the development of programmes, because teachers' focal concerns within all schools are much more related to those variables that are located at the classroom level, such as teaching, pedagogy and curriculum, than they are related to activities at the school level, like management and organisation. This is probably particularly the case in ineffective schools, where there may exist a majority of staff who define the role of the teacher very narrowly as being related to curriculum and instruction, rather than being more broadly related to school level management and organisational factors. It is clear that the neglect of the classroom level and the celebration of the school level may have historically cost us valuable teacher commitment.

• Multiple 'levers' are pulled to encourage school and teacher development, with the focus upon only the school 'owning' the process of change from the 1980s being replaced by a concern to utilise all reinforcers and initiators of change from outside the school (the local education authority or district), and indeed the national policy agenda to stimulate and provoke change.

• It has been clear that improvement programmes historically have not been necessarily organisationally 'tight'. Because of the fact that most of the programmes have been voluntaristic because they are linked to existing ongoing school level and individual level continuing professional development, it is clear that there may have been a huge differential within schools in the extent to which the programmes have been taken up. Reading between the lines, it is clear that there has been a likely tendency for programmes to impact most on the competent 'leading edge' of teachers, while it is also clear that a more or less significant 'trailing edge' may not have participated in the programmes, or at least may not have participated very fully. It is highly likely that there has been within schools participating in the programmes, therefore, a substantial variation in the extent to which they have permeated within schools and the extent to which organisational innovations have moved through to implementation from the initiation phase, and ultimately to the institutionalisation phase. Given there is increasing evidence within school effectiveness of the importance of organisational cohesion, consistency and constancy, as outlined in Chapter Three earlier, a situation in which there is greater variation between members of staff in a school because of differential take-up of improvement activities could have been adversely affecting the quality of student outcomes. The new range of programmes described in the following sections share commitments to enhanced *fidelity* of implementation, and to enhanced organisational *reliability* in the take-up of the various programme characteristics.

We proceed now to look at the new 'second wave' projects of the 1990s themselves.

HALTON'S EFFECTIVE SCHOOLS PROJECT IN CANADA

The Effective Schools Project in the Halton Board of Education in Ontario started, in 1986, as an attempt to bring the results of school effectiveness research carried out within Britain (Mortimore *et al.*, 1988) into the schooling practices of Canada, but it soon became clear that potential difficulties involved in the project's implementation could only be resolved by the adoption at school and system level of organisational and planning arrangements from the school improvement literature. Essentially, 'top-down' mandates to schools did not address the issues of ownership and commitment, nor did they pay attention to the process and impact of the changes upon those who worked to implement the policy mandates.

At the beginning of the project, a search of the international effectiveness literature was carried out by members of a task force, and a model of the characteristics of effectiveness was produced. Visits were undertaken to school districts where change was known to have occurred successfully, and meetings with the school improvement specialist Michael Fullan convinced task force members that improvement was more likely to occur if the school was seen as the focal point of change. A school growth planning process was developed, largely based on British models (McMahon *et al.*, 1984; ILEA, 1986), and similar to the school development plan that is now a feature of many countries, states and territories and which was outlined as a process in Chapter 4.

Where do the effective schools characteristics fit in? Within the assessment, or audit, phase, when the school is trying to get a picture of its current successes and areas for improvement, the staff examines Halton's model of characteristics as it relates to its own context. Questionnaires for teachers, students and parents focus on where respondents think the school is in relation to a set of indicators, and how important each indicator is in order to create a more effective school. Through analysing the gap between where the school is and where it should be, the school can identify areas of need. Furthermore, the information from the three sources provides triangulation. Clearly, this is not the only information schools examine during the assessment phase; they also look at current curricula and instructional practices, at initiatives coming out of the school board and the Ontario Ministry of Education, and also at a variety of information related to their students' progress and development. In line with the emphasis on equity in school effectiveness research, schools are encouraged to disaggregate student data, that is, to look for any differences in achievement, progress or development between subsets of the population.

Further understandings about school improvement have been gained during the project. The school growth planning process that has been adopted is very different from traditional forms of educational planning in Halton. Increased staff development in decision-making has necessitated greater understanding on the part of principals of the processes involved in working with groups. In the more successful schools, attention has been paid early on to the development of clear decision-making structures and organisational processes that will reduce later problems. In short, in these schools a climate has been built within which a more dynamic and ongoing planning process can occur. More importantly, time has been spent building a collaborative culture within the schools, in which teachers continue to learn and feel valued, and risk-taking is encouraged. Finally, teachers are encouraged to articulate their values and beliefs so that a shared vision for the school's future can be developed. In essence, the school growth planning process has shown that the creation of an effective school depends on more than the knowledge of what has been successful and effective elsewhere, although that can be a useful starting point.

Further important characteristics of this project have been the importance of the school district's role in the process. Halton created a strategic plan that emphasised three key directions. One of these was the growth planning process itself. The second, through a link with *The Learning Consortium* (Fullan *et al.*, 1990), was a focus on instruction, in recognition of the central role in the determination of school outcomes of what actually goes on in the classroom, the teaching and learning process. The third direction supported the other two, that is, an emphasis on staff development. Thus the system provided a framework within which growth planning could occur, and offered support for the process. This support came in the form of voluntary workshops for school teams on all aspects of growth planning, on a variety of instructional strategies and assessment, and for entire school staffs on their chosen instructional goals. Support was also offered through regional consultants who worked with individual teachers or whole staffs, and area consultants and special education staff assigned to particular schools. Thus the school was not seen as an isolated unit of change, but as the centre of change, connected to a wider system. This system also has to continue to grow, and in 1993, through a collaborative process involving representatives from the entire system as well as the local community, the three original directions were re-endorsed and a new one added, concerning the importance of the school system's relationship with its community.

Various effective school questionnaires were also used throughout the system to look at the impact of the project on attitudes, and data customarily used within effectiveness research such as student retention data were collected, and showed a decrease in dropouts over the six years of the project. Halton continues to perform above average on Ministry of Education curriculum reviews, and individual schools have demonstrated improvements in student attitudes and attendance, as well as on other specific indicators related to their specific growth plans.

Institutionalisation of school growth planning in Halton, another outcome of the project, resulted from the weaving together of a variety of initiatives; the development of a shared language around school effectiveness and school improvement; incorporation within the process of existing aspects of Halton's educational culture, such as the teacher evaluation process, and a strong commitment to collaboration; strategic directions that acknowledge the importance of the process; and an emphasis on well coordinated leadership and staff development (Stoll and Fink, 1996).

IMPROVING THE QUALITY OF EDUCATION FOR ALL (IQEA)

The IQEA school improvement project provides an interesting example of how a school improvement project can evolve and bridge between the first and second waves. What began as a whole school staff development initiative, over time transformed itself into a school improvement initiative with a total commitment to enhancing classroom practice.

The overall aim of IQEA is 'to produce and evaluate a model of school development, and a programme of support, that strengthens a school's ability to provide quality education for all its pupils by building upon existing good practice' (Hopkins *et al.*, 1994). In the project, approaches and methods from the improvement and effectiveness paradigms are blended; in particular, these include use of and work on improvement and change processes with input on school and classroom effectiveness and measurement of outcomes.

On the basis of their early pilot work in school improvement conducted within this study, Hopkins and his colleagues (Hopkins and Ainscow, 1993) outline five assumptions on which they based later phases of the project:

- School improvement is a process that focuses on enhancing the quality of students' learning.
- The vision of the school should be one which embraces all members of the school community as both learners and contributors.
- The school will see in external pressures for change important opportunities to secure its internal priorities.
- The school will seek to develop structures and create conditions which encourage collaboration and lead to the empowerment of individuals and groups.
- The school will seek to promote the view that monitoring and evaluation quality is a responsibility which all members of staff share.

The project, which began with only nine schools in 1991, has grown each year, and currently involves forty schools in several areas of the country. A contract is agreed between school staff, the Local Education Authority and the project team. All staff of a school have to agree that the school will participate, and at least 40 per cent receive release time to engage in specific project-related activities in their own and each other's classrooms, although all staff participate in certain IQEA-focused staff development events. At least two staff members are designated as coordinators and attend ten days of training and support meetings, for which accreditation is offered. The school selects its own priorities for development and its own methods to achieve these priorities. It also participates in the evaluation of the project and has to commit itself to share findings with other participants in the project.

The original conceptualisation of the project was based on the experience that effective change strategies focus not only on the implementation of centralised policies or chosen initiatives, but also on creating the conditions within schools that can sustain the teaching–learning process. From their work on the IQEA project, there were identified a series of conditions that underpinned the work of these successful schools (Hopkins and Ainscow, 1993). Broadly stated, the conditions are:

- Staff development
- Involvement
- Leadership
- Coordination
- Enquiry and reflection
- Collaborative planning.

As work continued with IQEA schools on the building of 'capacity' in these areas, the project personnel began to observe a number of factors influencing how particular conditions can best contribute to a 'moving school' ethos (Rosenholtz, 1989). As a consequence they began to develop a series of propositions about the relationship between the way a school approaches a particular condition and the impact of that condition on the school's capacity to hold the key to the establishing of a school culture which can meaningfully empower all teachers within the school community (Hopkins and West, 1994). The propositions are summarised in Table 6.1.

These six conditions and the related propositions were the focus of early work with the IQEA project schools. Subsequently, the project

Table 6.1 A framework for school improvement: some propositions

Proposition One
Schools will not improve unless teachers, individually and collectively, develop. While teachers can often develop their practice on an individual basis, if the whole school is to develop then there need to be many *staff development* opportunities for teachers to learn together.

Proposition Two
Successful schools seem to have ways of working that encourage feelings of *involvement* from a number of stakeholder groups, especially students.

Proposition Three
Schools that are successful at development establish a clear vision for themselves and regard *leadership* as a function to which many staff contribute, rather than a set of responsibilities vested in a single individual.

Proposition Four
The *coordination* of activities is an important way of keeping people involved, particularly when changes of policy are being introduced. Communication within the school is an important aspect of coordina-tion, as are the informal interactions that arise between teachers.

Proposition Five
Those schools which recognise that *enquiry and reflection* are important processes in school improvement find it easier to gain clarity and establish shared meanings around identified development priorities, and are better placed to monitor the extent to which policies actually deliver the intended outcomes for pupils.

Proposition Six
Through the *process of planning for development* the school is able to link its educational aspirations to identifiable priorities, sequence those priorities over time and maintain a focus on classroom practice.

Source: Hopkins and West, 1994

began to focus some of its research energies on to what was originally thought to be a parallel set of conditions which related to the notion of capacity at the classroom level. These conditions were connected to teacher development, much in the same way as the original set of conditions were connected to school development. As such, they were supposed to be transferable across classrooms and between teachers, and related to a variety of teaching–learning initiatives designed to enhance the achievement of students. At this stage, the project adapted a 'Framework for School Improvement' (Hopkins *et al.*,

1994) to express the relationship, as it then saw it, between school and classroom conditions, and the process of development in schools. The resulting conceptualisation looked something like Figure 6.1.

The first 'cut' of the classroom conditions was developed through discussion among the IQEA team at Cambridge and a series of day conferences with project schools. About twenty-five schools and a hundred teachers had an input into these early discussions. This is the initial list of classroom conditions which emerged from the deliberations:

- *Authentic relationships* – the quality, openness and congruence of relationships existing in the classroom.
- *Rules and boundaries* – the pattern of expectations set by the teacher and school of student performance and behaviour within the classroom.
- *Teacher's repertoire* – being the range of teaching styles and models internalised and available to a teacher on student, context, curriculum and desired outcome.
- *Reflection on teaching* – the capacity of the individual teacher to reflect on his/her own practice and to put to the test of practice specifications of teaching from other sources.
- *Resources and preparation* – the access of teachers to a range of pertinent teaching materials and the ability to plan and differentiate these materials for a range of students.
- *Pedagogic partnerships* – the ability of teachers to form professional relationships within the classroom that focus on the study and improvement of practice.

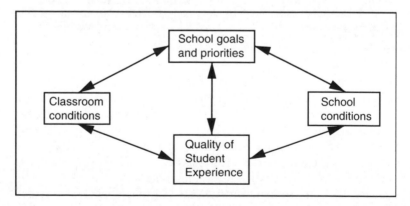

Figure 6.1 The relationship between school and classroom conditions

The IQEA project personnel believe that these conditions are the key to facilitating effective teaching and high quality outcomes at the classroom or learning levels, in just the same way that the other conditions potentiate high quality outcomes at the school level.

THE LEWISHAM SCHOOL IMPROVEMENT PROJECT IN LONDON

The Lewisham School Improvement Project commenced in the spring of 1993 and arose out of a partnership between Lewisham schools, Lewisham Local Education Authority (LEA) and the University of London Institute of Education. It has four aims:

- to enhance pupil progress, achievement and development;
- to develop the internal capacity of schools for managing change and evaluating its impact at:
  - whole school level;
  - classroom level;
  - student level;
- to develop the capacity of the LEA to provide data to schools that will strengthen their ability to plan and evaluate change;
- to integrate the above with the system's ongoing in-service and support services to form a coherent approach to professional development.

The project has six dimensions, although these overlap to some extent:

1 *Leadership development* – a series of voluntary five-day workshops ('Leaders Together') with head teachers and deputy head teachers across the borough of Lewisham, who work with a partner during and between sessions. Topics covered include and emphasise the importance of leadership and management of school effectiveness and school improvement.

2 *School projects* – more intensive work with an initial pilot group of ten schools (primary, secondary and special schools are represented), the heads and deputies of whom have participated in the initial workshops. A second group of schools has subsequently been involved. These schools have identified a focus for improvement and learning, and cross-role project teams attend several sessions in which they work with Institute facilitators to refine their focus areas through analysis of school-based data. They are also

introduced to the school effectiveness and school improvement research findings, with a special emphasis on their role as change agents within their schools. The title of the workshop series, 'Moving Together', reflects the positive impact on school improvement of teachers learning together (Rosenholtz, 1989). Accreditation has been offered for course and project work.

There were nine 'ground rules' for participation in this part of the project, formulated on assessment of the findings of school effectiveness and school improvement research.

(a) There is a focus on achievement in its broadest sense to ensure that the core of the project emphasises outcomes for pupils, and teaching and learning. Examination of school effectiveness findings and the notion of 'value-added' (Thomas *et al.*, 1995) has helped schools to focus their efforts on this.

(b) The project follows the edict to 'Start small, think big', so that the focus of the project is manageable and linked to the school's development plan, in recognition that school development and classroom development go hand in hand (Fullan and Hargreaves, 1991; Hargreaves and Hopkins, 1991).

(c) The project involves teams of people and emphasises the importance of shared leadership and teacher ownership in school improvement.

(d) The project highlights the composition of teams, in order that teams who coordinate the project in their school and attend workshops should represent the entire staff in their composition, and may also include other stakeholders.

(e) The project believes the teams are agents of change. While the school improvement teams are not responsible for change in their school, they need to facilitate that change, and therefore must understand the change process and its impact on people.

(f) The project is school-managed and it is the school's responsibility to establish and maintain their project's focus, to manage the change process and to monitor and evaluate the project (van Velzen *et al.*, 1985).

(g) There is systematic monitoring and evaluation, and the project acknowledges the importance of setting success criteria, gathering and evaluating evidence, and using the knowledge and information gained.

(h) There is support from outside the school from the LEA in the form of advisory services, tailor-made staff development programmes, access to present programmes, resourcing, and help with measurement of indicators of achievement and development. Support from the Institute of Education focuses on strengthening the school's capacity to manage change effectively, through accredited training and visits to individual schools.

(i) The project is concerned with dissemination – project schools are involved in disseminating their findings to colleagues throughout the school system.

3 *Indicators creation* – a voluntary group of fifteen teachers, head-teachers, LEA advisers and officers have identified and developed LEA and whole school indicators of change, development and achievement, with a focus on pupils with special educational needs. These indicators will be available to schools when evaluating their effectiveness in respect of individual pupils' progress, whole school systems and value for money. They will also provide data to inform the LEA's strategic planning, including its resourcing and moni-toring role.

4 *Monitoring and evaluation* – evaluation of change is fundamental to the project, and the question 'Has it made a difference?' is a recurring theme. The intention is for the project itself to exemplify appropriate evaluation procedures and to demonstrate effective-ness, as well as encouraging and supporting schools to evaluate their own effectiveness.

The LEA collects borough-wide data on examination results, attendance and truancy, exclusions and staff absence data, broken down by gender and ethnicity for each school. Pupil baseline data at age 11 also include the London Reading Test and a group reading test to be completed by all pupils during their first month in secondary school and are supplemented by a complementary test at the end of their first year. The available data will enable evaluation of the project's effectiveness in the pilot secondary schools against LEA averages, against other matched schools, and longitudinally. Some similar data exist for primary aged pupils. At present, however, the capacity for monitoring and evaluating effectiveness in primary schools is limited, and pilot primary schools are being assisted to develop appropriate indicators (Stoll and Thomson, 1996).

The Halton Effective Schools teacher survey (Stoll, 1992) has been adapted to be completed by staff in all the pilot schools and in a group of matched schools. It will be repeated after two years. The schools themselves also provide regular progress reports, addressing issues relating to success criteria, baseline data and progress to date.

An Institute researcher has carried out interviews in pilot schools, and LEA Link advisers completed questionnaires on their perspective of individual schools' progress. Interviews have also been carried out with key members of the LEA, including the director. Follow-up interviews are planned.

More recent school progress reports demonstrate the increased emphasis on changing classroom practice and opportunities for student learning. For example, in an update in September 1994 the deputy head teacher of the special school observed that the first year was largely devoted to the groundwork of staff-centred input and involvement, and teaching and assessment strategy development. This year, with these structures in place, the focus has shifted to students in the classroom.

One of the schools involved in the more detailed project work is a special school that caters for students who have severe learning difficulties and are between the ages of 11 and 19 years. The school has reported that 'Leaders Together' has provided them with the impetus to work as a staff to write novel curriculum group-based schemes of work. For their project they have chosen to focus on reporting and assessment in order to develop a system that will both support the UK's National Curriculum and allow for the marked differentiation between students that exists in their school. Part of the cultural conditions of the school which they also wish to incorporate into the project is the involvement of their non-teaching staff.

A primary school also involved in the project has concentrated on students' writing, the curriculum focus from the school's development plan. The staff as a whole have already spent time articulating their vision and aims for the school, and they have explored and coordinated a variety of strategies that include: analysis of the school's own statistics on achievement; using relevant research findings to inform practice; paired classroom observations; staff development sessions; yearly targets for individual teachers related to the aims of the project; and the development of a commonly known and agreed monitoring scheme to be used by the head teacher and languages teacher when they visit classrooms and give feedback to teachers.

5 *Governors and effectiveness* – more recent parallel work with governing bodies of several schools who have been introduced to

school effectiveness and school improvement issues and are working through them as they relate to their own role in promoting greater school effectiveness.

6 *Dissemination* – dissemination within and beyond the LEA takes place. The last two annual head and deputy head conferences have taken school improvement as their theme. Schools and their LEA partners also share experiences and understandings gained locally, around the country and in other LEAs, at Institute of Education conferences, and national and international research conferences. A presentation to the International Congress for School Effectiveness and Improvement on the work of the project included the three partners in the project: the Institute, the LEA and the schools.

SCHOOLS MAKE A DIFFERENCE (SMAD) IN HAMMERSMITH AND FULHAM, LONDON

In early 1993, Hammersmith and Fulham LEA established the *Schools Make a Difference* Project to help the borough's eight secondary schools raise student levels of attainment, achievement and morale (Myers, 1995). While affiliation to the project was optional, all eight schools in the authority chose to participate. The project's guiding principles were based on school effectiveness research findings. These principles were:

- that students need to believe that schooling can be worthwhile and relevant;
- that learning must be challenging and relevant, to encourage students to develop their capabilities as responsible, thoughtful and active citizens;
- that students' intellectual, personal and technical abilities, aptitudes and capabilities are recognised and valued, and that expectations of progress and performance are high;
- that good behaviour is a necessary condition for effective learning, and that students take responsibility for their own behaviour and display a high level of engagement in a well structured learning process;
- that parental involvement is vital and should be sought;
- that all staff in the schools are involved in, and committed to, the school's development;
- that schools and the community work towards a shared vision and that a professional learning community is created within schools;

- that headteachers have a vital role to play in providing a climate where this can occur;
- that a 'plan, do and review' approach is systematically and rigorously applied.

Hammersmith and Fulham LEA appointed a project manager to work with schools and LEA personnel to establish the structures and procedures for the project. Within her role she made regular visits to the schools and took the schools' senior management teams to visit schools of interest around the country. In conjunction with head teachers and higher education staff, she has also organised in-service training for the coordinators, head teachers, senior management teams and various other staff members.

The schools all appointed project coordinators, who were awarded thirty half days of 'cover' by other staff in order to carry out work associated with the project in their schools, attend in-service training sessions and visit other schools. Coordinators receive accreditation for their course and project work through the London Institute of Education. The coordinators established project working parties in their schools that included representation from a wide range of teaching and support staff and, in some schools, from students, parents and governors.

Each school produced a project plan based on criteria agreed by the head teachers for expenditure of the project budget. The plan was developed as a result of wide consultation, and included a project focus based on the school's development plan. Several schools chose as a focus flexible learning strategies, and engaged in a variety of forms of staff development to help introduce new teaching and student study methods to staff. In one school, for example, the eight voluntary members of the SMAD Development Group decided to pair up with a partner to engage in classroom observation and act as each other's 'critical friend'. Supply cover for this has been incorporated within the school's project plan. The project also funded school-based revision centres during the Easter vacation that have already helped increase student engagement.

The project's findings, as highlighted by its external evaluator (Pocklington, 1995) were that, while there was an overall rise in student achievement across all of the schools in 1993–94, differing rates of progress were achieved across the eight schools. Although it is difficult to ascribe improvement to particular aspects of the project, likely contributors were examination revision centres and coursework clinics, celebratory events, an emphasis in most schools on student consultation, students' responses to improvements to the physical environment, and 'the beginnings of transforming the dominant ethos in the pupil sub-culture' (Pocklington, 1995: 125).

Four factors appeared to bear significantly on the extent to which the project was successful in each school:

- hiring of a virtually full-time project manager;
- appointment of a coordinator in each school;
- partnership between the coordinator and head teacher;
- establishment of a group in each school to facilitate and oversee project implementation.

THE BARCLAY–CALVERT PROJECT IN THE UNITED STATES

Our discussion here about this project, and especially about the relationship between school effectiveness and school improvement, is based on a four-year evaluation (Stringfield *et al.*, 1995). In this project the curricular and instructional package of Calvert, a private school in Baltimore, is being implemented in Barclay, an inner-city public school in the same city. The Calvert school offers a kindergarten through grade six day school programme to a predominantly highly affluent clientele in Baltimore. Since early this century, the school has also offered a highly structured, certified home study curriculum. Procedures for the teachers' provision of lessons, parent/school contact, and evaluation standards for each unit of the curriculum are all unusually specific. Each grade's curriculum and instructional program is provided in a level of detail that often approximates to scripting. Moreover, the entire programme places an unusually high emphasis on student-generated products. Students generate 'folders' of work that are regularly reviewed by their teacher, their parents, and the school's administrators. According to the evaluation team, the curriculum itself is not revolutionary but reflects decades of high and academically traditional demands, blended with an emphasis on the importance of classwork and homework and an intensive writing programme. All the work undertaken by students reflects the characteristics of effective teaching, linked together with a high achievement level of the intakes. It is thus easy to understand why the results on norm-referenced achievement tests are very good. Virtually every grade of the select population of Calvert students score above the 90th percentile when compared to public, elite suburban and private school norms.

By contrast, Barclay School is a kindergarten through grade eight public school in Baltimore. The population served by Barclay is 94 per cent minority. Nearly 80 per cent of the students attending Barclay School receive free or reduced price lunch. The neighbourhood is one of old factories and terraced houses. The school serves some families led by drug dealers, prostitutes, or less well off graduate students at Johns Hopkins University; however, the great majority of students are the children of working class or unemployed African–Americans, often from single-parent families. In the late 1980s it became clear that the school's achievement scores were poor, as well as the attendance rate and levels of student discipline in the classrooms and school halls. So, Barclay could be seen as having the typical problems of an inner-city American school.

The principal at Barclay became interested in the Calvert School programme and the two schools developed a proposal to implement the entire Calvert programme at Barclay School. The programme was to be implemented by the Barclay staff. The staff would receive training in the Calvert philosophy, materials, and instructional system. Ongoing staff development would be provided by a facilitator who had both public school and Calvert teaching experience.

Implementation began in the autumn of 1990 in kindergarten at first grade. Each year one additional grade has been added. For two weeks each summer the Barclay–Calvert facilitator trains the next grade's Barclay teachers in the Calvert philosophy, curriculum and methods. The facilitator spends the school year working with each succeeding group of teachers in an effort to maximise the chance of full programme implementation.

The key factors making for the project's success are argued to be:

1 Having funding

The funding of the programme by a private foundation made it possible to appoint a full-time coordinator who acted as the project facilitator. It should be noted, however, that the entire four-year grant has supplied less money than is the annual difference in total funding between a disadvantaged Baltimore City and a suburban Baltimore County school. One of the benefits of this was that everything needed for instruction was there on time in a sufficient quantity (one of the major disadvantages at Barclay School in the past).

2 Having non-fiscal support

The funding foundation was involved in the programme, not only in fiscal decisions, but also in regular staff meetings and in efforts to anticipate and solve problems. Barclay's principal was highly talented and very determined to make the programme a success. She visited classes, attended meetings and was very active in involving parents. Furthermore, the Calvert coordinator at Barclay was very supportive with respect to the implementation, and brought high levels of knowledge, competence and enthusiasm to the programme implementation. Another source of support was Calvert School itself. The head teacher remained a supporter of the project; he assisted Barclay School, visited classrooms and repeatedly made himself available for consultations. Finally, the parents of Barclay were very actively involved at every stage of the project.

3 Having an achievable plan

The Barclay–Calvert project was very methodical. Barclay did not attempt to implement the whole Calvert curriculum and instructional programme all at once, but gradually, grade level by grade level. In this way it was possible to prepare teachers for the next grade level, utilising a cascade model.

4 Having a high quality curriculum

The curriculum itself involves five processes that are extremely important for its success.

(a) Students read a lot (that means increasing opportunity to learn).
(b) All students produce a lot of work.
(c) Teachers check students' work and also correct all their own work.
(d) Student folders are read by the coordinator, the principal or the Calvert administrator every month. Therefore, student monitoring is very strong.
(e) The student folders are sent home every month, which increases parent involvement in what students do and also in checking homework.

5 Having positive teacher attitudes

It is striking in Calvert School that teachers are highly confident that Calvert students can excel academically. It was one of the major changes of the implementation of the Calvert programme in Barclay that the teacher attitudes changed also at Barclay. They were convinced that the Calvert programme was helping them to teach more, teach better, and to help more children perform at higher levels. These are not of course unrealistic expectations, since the teachers have good grounds for their optimistic beliefs, because they have received meaningful, ongoing support and because they were observing enhanced results.

6 Emphasising classroom instruction

Little changes in students' academic achievement unless something changes between the student, the curriculum and the instruction. The Calvert programme is reaching towards the student, for which there are several reasons.

First, the curriculum has been put in place. The curriculum demands high fidelity implementation. Second, a high quality instructional system is also in place. Almost all the teachers have made significant changes in their teaching and have become more effective. In classroom observation, it turned out that the student 'on-task' rates in the Barclay–Calvert classes were often very high and that teachers reported that, given high quality instruction and instructional support, the Barclay students were responding well to the raised demands. In summary, the Calvert programme has enjoyed a far better chance of achieving full implementation than most novel programmes in school systems.

In the evaluation of the programme, student testing was also included. The data from norm-referenced achievement testing programmes indicate that students in the programme are achieving academically at a rate significantly above their pre-programme Barclay School peers. This finding is consistent across reading, writing, and mathematics, and is particularly striking in writing. The Barclay students are also making progress not only in specific areas of academic content, but also in their ability to integrate new material and absorb new knowledge. Additional data indicate that the Barclay–Calvert project has reduced student absences, reduced student transfers from the school, greatly reduced the number of students requiring special education services, reduced diagnosis and referrals on the grounds of 'learning disablement', eliminated disciplinary removals, and increased the number of students found eligible for the Gifted and Talented Education (GATE) programme. Taken collectively, the diverse measures indicate a very successful school improvement project which, above all, has been reliably implemented.

THE DUTCH NATIONAL SCHOOL IMPROVEMENT PROJECT

The National School Improvement Project (NSIP) was carried out in the Netherlands, began in 1991/92, and continued for three years. Preliminary results were reported in 1995 (Houtveen and Osinga, 1995).

A major goal of the NSIP was to reduce, and if possible prevent, educational disadvantage, especially in reading. The background of the study was that there are clear differences between schools in effectiveness, especially with respect to student performance in the basic skills of language and reading. The school improvement project makes use of the knowledge base of school effectiveness research, especially the insights given by school effectiveness research into the factors that correlate with student performance. Special attention has also been given to instructional and management factors at the classroom level and to the conditional and contingent factors of management and organisation at the school level.

The project also makes use of the knowledge base developed in other Dutch school improvement projects, of which some were based on effectiveness research. This is especially important, because these type of projects in the Netherlands have been shown to be less effective in the past. Maybe the goals of these past projects were too ambitious. Another reason for their failure could be the lack of attention to the quality of instruction and management at the classroom level. The Dutch National Improvement Project aims to learn from these past projects and particularly to ensure that support given by external agencies should be directed to the factors at the classroom and school levels that contribute to student outcomes.

An external evaluation of the project has been necessary, but these researchers have also provided information that is useful for focusing and monitoring of the project itself. The goals of the project can be divided into those at the classroom or teacher level and those at the school level. At the classroom level, the following objectives are aimed at being realised:

- Improving teachers' skills in the field of direct instruction;
- Improving teachers' skills in the field of group management, generating an efficient use of time by the pupils;
- Promotion of teachers' expertise concerning rigorous and methodical working;

- Using effective principles of instruction, with regard to technical reading.

At the school level, the following targets are being aimed at:

- To realise a 'results-oriented' school management in which concrete targets concerning basic skills at school and group levels are determined in advance;
- Increasing the evaluation capacity of the school, in connection with the previous point, by:
    regular and reliable evaluation of individual pupils' achievements with the help of a pupil 'tracking' system;
    making a valid analysis of the teaching activities and the organisational characteristics of the school with the help of a school diagnosis instrument.

The key features of the project are obviously closely related to the project's goals:

- The main focus of the project is on the improvement of education at the classroom level to increase the level of effective instruction. But effective instruction at the classroom level depends on management at the classroom level and upon the different factors and characteristics at the school and the above school levels. So, the first concern of the project is ensuring that the school policy at the different levels is achievement-oriented. This holds for the classroom, school and board or governor level, and includes parents.
- The project reflects the belief that the prevention of reading failure can be achieved by improving the instructional behaviour of teachers.
- The support, internal and external, should be directed towards enhancing the practice-oriented professionalism of teachers and school management. This means that it is not only aimed at knowledge-transfer but also at coaching and putting improvement into practice, which is also given attention in the project. This means that the project's goals are clear, that it has a predetermined time-span, and that it also has a predetermined set of activities.

The programme itself has specific features that are based on the findings of educational research:

- Methodical working, which means that all pupils are regularly tested. In this way a data base on groups of students, and individual students in the classroom, is available, on which decisions with respect to the entire group, or to individual students, can be made. Also, the monitoring of students' progress is rigorous in this programme. The management of the school plays an initiating, coordinating and supervising role.

- Direct instruction as a basic principle of teaching (with the following important phases: evaluation on a daily basis; a clear presentation of the new content or skills; supervised exercise and individual application of knowledge).
- Structured courses inculcating methods for initial reading.
- Increasing instructional and effective learning time (connected with the emphasis upon direct instruction).
- Teaching climate, which is to be made positive for students and includes the generation of experiences of success, of positive expectations of teachers towards learning and students' possibilities, and of teachers' confidence in their own possibilities of influence on student results.

The support strategy in the project consists of a combination of multiple elements, like informing the school board, consultation with principals, guidance at the level of the team of teachers, and coaching of teachers in the classroom.

In the project evaluation, two main questions with respect to the NSIP are being answered:

1 Does the guidance programme result in an increase in effective teaching, more direct instruction, an increase in the use of the effective methods for teaching reading and an increase in methodical working?
2 Do their teaching behaviours result in an improvement of pupil results in technical reading?

In the evaluation study, twenty-nine schools were included, sixteen of which belonged to the 'experimental' group and thirteen to the 'control' group. With respect to task-oriented learning and instruction time, direct instruction, methodical working and teaching reading according to effective methods, it can be concluded that the strategy used in this project has been successful, since there is a considerable growth in the experimental group over a period of two-and-a-half years.

In the student achievement study, 319 students were involved in the experimental group and 137 in the control group. These groups were tested in March 1993 (some months before the school year 1993/94), and in June 1994. There was a correction for intake for individual pupil characteristics like initial ability, socio-economic background and attitudes towards reading. After correction for the pre-test and student characteristics, there is a significant effect in favour of the experimental group over the control group upon student achievement in reading.

It can be concluded that the improvement strategy used in the National School Improvement Project, which was based on a knowledge base with respect to school effectiveness and successful school improvement projects, and the programme content itself, based on a knowledge base with respect to educational effectiveness and instructional effectiveness (especially in the area of initial reading), turns out to be effective. The planned change strategy leads to changes in teaching behaviour, and the students in the experimental group involved in the programme based on educational effectiveness outperform students in the control group.

THE HIGHLY RELIABLE SCHOOL PROJECT IN THE UNITED KINGDOM

This recent project was born from Stringfield's (1995) suggestion that educational systems had much to learn from the organisational processes of those firms and utilities that were not permitted to fail. These are known in the jargon of the trade as HROs or High Reliability Organisations. They are usually taken to be air traffic controllers, nuclear power plant operatives, electricity supply operatives, and all those other organisations and their employees who have to generate 100 per cent reliable functioning (see Stringfield and Slavin, 1991).

The project in its promotional material frequently utilises aircraft analogies, arguing, for example, that if one is in a holding pattern above Heathrow Airport, it is not reassuring to note that one has the technology to land the plane but might not use it, or that only 30 per cent of air traffic controllers are effective air traffic controllers, or that we are trying to do something by understanding the ineffective air traffic controllers but have not quite managed it yet! Because of the cost, both human and financial, of any failure, the plane must land. Recent estimates suggest the cost of avoidable school failure within the United States to be the equivalent of a plane crash every week, yet little is done to prevent school failure and much is done to prevent air traffic controller failure.

The characteristics of these HROs have been determined to be as follows:

- they train extensively, pre-service and in-service, in order to eliminate operational flaws. When training, all levels of an organisation act as respondents on the effectiveness of all levels, in a process of mutual monitoring;
- the goals of the HROs are few and explicit (the job of the air traffic controller is to land the plane, not to relate socially to the pilot!);
- there is a body of knowledge about practice that is codified into SOPs – Standard Operating Procedures – which tell people how to behave in the event of any contingency;
- great attention is given to minor errors, since the belief is that these could cascade into major system failure;
- simulations to identify weak links are always being run, with direct action being taken to identify the trailing edge and to make it more effective;
- the organisations are well resourced, and equipment is kept in good order.

Underlying the reasons for the existence of all the organisational procedures is the belief that system failure or unreliability would generate costs that are too heavy for a society to bear.

With eight secondary schools, working in close association with Sam Stringfield of Johns Hopkins University in the United States and David Reynolds of Newcastle University's Department of Education, a programme has been developed to model schools on these highly reliable organisations from other fields outside education. The programme consists of the following:

- All the schools have joined a performance indicator system that generates high quality data upon student achievement, the ALIS ('A' Level Information System) and YELLIS (Year Eleven Information System) schemes pioneered by Fitz-Gibbon and colleagues at the University of Newcastle upon Tyne (Fitz-Gibbon, 1992). These data feed back to schools their relative performance on their different public examination subjects, and relate directly to the effectiveness of their departments.
- All the schools are testing their intake of new pupils as they arrive from junior school. The testing will be repeated at the beginning of each school year, for these pupils plus for the new intake of pupils. Ultimately all pupils will be tested annually. These data will reveal

those pupils who have unrealised potential, plus a 'gain score' will be provided for each year that will be a baseline.

- The schools will be provided with the best knowledge available as their standard operating practices. Schools make available two of their five in-service days each year for 'HRS' activities. One day will be for a formal knowledge input of school effectiveness/school improvement knowledge. The other day will be for an input of teacher effectiveness knowledge, plus in both days some skilling of whole school staffs. Both days will be oriented around background pre-reading, formal presentations and more group related activities.

- Schools are to adopt up to four goals to be their 'HRS' goals. Two project-wide goals will be academic achievement (e.g. percentage of students with five or more GCSEs at grade A–C, staying on rate, percentage of students with five or more GCSEs at grade A–G, plus GNVQ outcomes as appropriate), and the unauthorised absence rate. Up to two other goals, which must permit measurement, will also be chosen by each school to reflect school needs, priorities, developmental status etc.

- Schools are now generating between two and four (final) targets for the goals to be attained by the end of the 1999–2000 school year, with goals and (intermediate) targets for 1997–98. These will be very ambitious goals, as befits an ambitious project, but will also take account of what schools' differing 'start points' may be. The school targets, therefore, represent a move towards greater effectiveness by comparison with the start point.

Schools will then forward-map (from their intake) and backward-map (from GCSEs) the path necessary for a student to obtain five or more A–Cs. Progress along these maps will be closely monitored, and the maps themselves revised annually as schools gather actual testing and process data.

- Schools are developing new mechanisms to ensure the progress of the HRS year towards their goals, and are paying attention to the whole school. In particular, the necessity of mechanisms to prevent any 'trailing edge' of low achieving/disaffected pupils is being addressed. These could vary according to the social context of the schools, in accordance with the professional judgement of teachers in each school, built upon the objective testing. Focus groups of past pupils, with their parents, are being interviewed. Continuous collections of portfolios across subjects are being utilised. Questionnaires to pupils coming into school (and their parents) are also being utilised. Activities with primary feeder schools may also be tried. It is accepted that these mechanisms would vary by school, within the overall philosophy agreed by all project schools.

- There will be a focus upon improving departmental effectiveness. Once during the first year, and twice a year thereafter, each department will examine the academic products of all HRS students for a brief (two-week) period. The purpose will be to determine the extent to which all students are progressing. To the extent to which significant numbers of students are not making adequate progress, the department and administration will make suggestions for changes in those students' academic programmes (the focus of this work is also to relate to the UK's core National Curriculum objectives in each subject).

In this benchmarking against the good departments, the project will be distinctive in that:

- the focus will be on the students' regular work, plus observation of classrooms and teaching in different departments;
- the psychological processes involved in these various difficult issues will be given very careful consideration.

The overall theme of the programme is as follows:

- *Year One*   schools receive the most valuable knowledge from research about effective practices and develop 'data rich' environments that will give fine-grained analyses of where individual pupils are and of where individual departments are. The departments begin to be organised around quality issues. The schools begin to develop mechanisms to eradicate failure.
- *Year Two*   schools begin to focus upon, and learn from, their own best practice identified in the data on their departments. More data, on more years of pupils, becomes available. The in-service activities from outside move more to the 'skilling' of the schools to generate their own knowledge.
- *Year Three*   schools begin to learn from best practice outside themselves, in other project schools and in other schools not in the project.

The project team believe that the results will be dramatically improved pupil achievements and dramatically improved school quality.

TOWARDS THIRD WAVE PROJECTS

We noted in the Introduction to this chapter that 'second wave' projects of the 1990s had several differences by comparison with 'first wave' projects of the 1980s. They have:

- focused more closely on classrooms and have been more prepared to utilise teacher effectiveness literature;
- been concerned to 'pull all relevant levers' by operating with the outside-school, school and classroom levels simultaneously;
- been concerned to address 'reliability' issues, as well as issues of validity, by ensuring that innovations are reliably spread throughout project schools, to ensure cohesion and consistency;
- been concerned to relate programmes very closely to the findings of the existing research base, both in being conceptually rigorous in their use of that material and being sure that there is 'fidelity' in the implementation of the programmes and the research literature.

If we were to consider what might be the further directions in which the newly merged effectiveness/improvement enterprise might go, some possibilities suggest themselves.

Context-specific school improvement

We clearly need to develop more 'contextually specific' school improvement strategies, in which we tailor the precise nature of the programmes offered to the 'presenting culture' and context of individual schools. If we were to summarise our likely 'third wave' projects, they would have the following programme contents:

- an audit of existing classroom and school processes and outcomes, and comparison with desired end states (particularly focusing upon the educational experiences of different pupil groups);
- generation of knowledge about what to change at both an organisational and a cultural level from scanning best existing practice within the school, in other schools and from the research literature;
- creation of an infrastructure to get the knowledge base taken up, involving use of the levels of the school and outside-school agencies;
- evaluation of the effect of changes upon academic and social outcomes and processes;
- a distinctive focus upon classrooms and student learning, as well as upon school conditions that facilitate this.

'Third wave' initiatives would clearly also be of both quantitative and qualitative methodology, of both 'top down' pressure and 'bottom up' support to provide change, and of both knowledge from practice and knowledge from research.

It is important, though, to add a further dimension to these characteristics, namely a knowledge generating capacity or 'learning school' capacity at individual school level. The necessity for this is due to the following factors.

- It is highly unlikely that there will ever be a knowledge base produced outside schools that will be absolutely appropriate for each individual school. If what is necessary for effectiveness varies partially by context, it is highly unlikely that effectiveness research can provide, from outside the school, knowledge appropriate according to the school's nation; socio-economic context; phase of internal development; urban/rural status; age phase; cultural conditions; educational personalities involved (to note but a few of the factors).
- The time scale of the research enterprise, with up to five years needed before a cohort of pupils passes through British secondary schools, for example, means that whatever research knowledge is produced may be redundant and out of date by the time that schools receive it.
- The pace of educational change means that knowledge obtained from schools under one set of educational arrangements may be invalid under another.

Most important of all, if the knowledge about 'good' or 'effective' practice comes from outside the school, then there may develop a dependency upon outsiders and an inability to truly construct a 'learning organisation' which produces its own educational knowledge.

From all this we can conclude that what is needed to develop schools are *combinations* of improvement and effectiveness practices and strategies appropriate to the nature of individual schools. For a school that is 'ineffective' and just starting the process of development, the strategies may be different from a school that has been developing over some time: the former may need an 'apprenticeship' orientation involving giving the school knowledge from outside, while the latter may be sufficiently professionally competent to generate its own good practice and the development based upon it. Likewise, the strategies would be different for an individual school at different phases of the development cycle, with beginning provision of information from outside being progressively scaled down until the school is capable of its own knowledge generation.

Hopkins (1996) has distinguished between three possible different 'Types' of strategies, for schools to focus upon in different contexts:

- *Type I* strategies are those that assist failing schools to become moderately effective. They need to involve a high level of external support, since failing schools cannot improve themselves. These strategies have to involve a clear and direct focus on a limited number of basic curriculum and organisational issues in order to build the confidence and competence to continue. Two examples of this directive, externally initiated, approach to school improvement would be the IBIS scheme developed by Hargreaves in the then ILEA (Hargreaves, 1990), or the Schenley High School experiment in school improvement in Pittsburgh (Wallace *et al.*, 1990).
- *Type II* strategies are those that assist moderately effective schools to become effective. These schools need to refine their developmental priorities to focus on specific teaching and learning issues, and to build the capacity within the school to support this work. These strategies usually involve a certain level of external support, but it is theoretically possible for schools in this category to 'improve' by themselves. It may therefore be more helpful to differentiate between 'Type IIa' and 'Type IIb' strategies. Type IIa strategies are characterised by a strategic focus on innovations in teaching and learning that are informed and supported by external knowledge and support. Examples of such school improvement strategies would be Joyce's 'Models of Teaching' approach (Joyce *et al.* , 1993, 1995). Type IIb strategies rely less on external support and tend to be more school-initiated. Strategic school improvement programmes, such as the 'Improving the Quality of Education for All' (IQEA) project referred to earlier (Hopkins *et al.* 1994), and the 'improvement through planning' approach recently described by the school inspectors in England and Wales (OFSTED, 1994), are pertinent examples.
- *Type III* strategies are those that assist effective schools to remain so. In these instances external support, although often welcomed, is not necessary as the school searches out and creates its own support networks. Exposure to new ideas and practices, collaboration through consortia or 'pairing' type arrangements, seem to be

common in these situations. Examples of these types of school improvement strategies would be those described by Myers and Stoll (1993) in the UK, and school improvement projects such as the 'League of Professional Schools' (Glickman, 1990) or the *Coalition of Essential Schools* (Sizer, 1992) in the USA.

Transformation in the 'culture' of schools

The second major direction for 'third wave' projects is to impact upon the 'culture of the school', an enduring theme in the literature on school effectiveness, improvement and change, as Sarason (1982) so evocatively captured in the title of his book *The Culture of the School and the Problem of Change*. In the same way as Rutter and his colleagues (1979) referred to the 'ethos' of the school as the unifying element of school effectiveness, Andy Hargreaves (1992) and Susan Rosenholtz (1989) refer to it as a crucial factor in school improvement. More recently David Hargreaves (1995) has attempted a fusion of effectiveness and improvement utilising the notion of culture. It is beyond the scope of this book to engage in a conceptual or empirical analysis of culture, although it is worth adding that this important work still needs to be done. It is appropriate, however, to conclude this book with a comment on the culture of the school and its relationship to school effectiveness and school improvement.

Many research studies have found that, without a period of destabilisation, successful, long-lasting change is unlikely to occur (Fullan, 1991). Yet it is at this point that most change fails to progress beyond early implementation. In these cases, when the change hits the 'wall' of individual learning or institutional resistance, turbulence begins to occur and development work begins to stall. The working group usually continues to meet for a while, but it generally backs off from focusing on classroom practice and requesting organisational modifications, and eventually progress slows. The change circles back on itself and nothing much is achieved – so we start something new. Fortunately, in our change-rich environment, another priority is soon found or another group emerges to focus on! This is the cycle of educational failure, the predictable pathology of educational change.

Many schools survive this period of destabilisation by either consciously or intuitively adapting their *internal conditions* (referred to in Chapter Four) to meet the demands of the agreed change or priority. When this happens, changes occur to the *culture* of the school. For example, classroom observation becomes more common in many schools as a result of development work. When this happens, teachers also begin to talk more about teaching, collaborative work outside of the particular project increases, and management structures are adapted to support the work. When taken together, these changes in attitudes, practice and structure create a more supportive environment within the school for managing change. The school's 'change capacity' is increased and the groundwork is laid for future change efforts. A virtuous circle of change begins to be established. Schools who have been through similar 'change cycles' either experience less internal turbulence, or are able to tolerate greater levels of turbulence, because they have progressively enhanced their capacity to change as a result of this developmental process. The link between school effectiveness/school improvement strategies and the culture of the school is therefore of crucial importance.

CONCLUSIONS – THE END OF ONE JOURNEY AND THE BEGINNING OF ANOTHER

We have journeyed widely in this volume through very large literatures and bodies of knowledge, and we hope that in our final Chapters Five and Six we have created some new knowledge of our own. What were two separate bodies of knowledge, with their own methodologies and conceptualisations, we have argued should become one. Whereas the existing paradigms have been created because of semi-philosophical and epistemological commitments among researchers which have generated certain bodies of knowledge and working practices, our approach here has been a more problem-centred one, in which we 'back-map' from the 'problem' of less than adequate educational standards to the means necessary to improve them. Education, we would argue, has been bedevilled by persons seeking educational practices that reflect a distinctive philosophy – we would prefer to leave philosophical arguments about the nature of the desirable knowledge and practices of schooling until we have more efficient delivery mechanisms, since there is little point debating what should be within school experience if schools are so ineffective and unimproved that they cannot adequately deliver *any* experiences with certainty of success.

It is the 'technology' or 'means' of schooling that we have therefore tried to build in the journey of this book, both in our codifying of existing knowledge and in our attempt to generate understanding of 'new waves' that are evident in the educational currents of the 1990s.

In all of this, it is clear that school effectiveness and school improvement can productively come together, for, as Cardina! Newman so accurately noted some considerable time ago, 'The truth does not lie midway between extremes but *in* both of them'.

REFERENCES

Barber, M., Denning, T., Gough, G. and Johnson, M. (1996) 'Urban education initiatives: the national pattern', in M. Barber and R. Dann (eds), *Raising Educational Standards in the Inner Cities: Practical Initiatives in Action*, London: Cassell.

Cotton, K. (1995) *Effective School Practices: A Research Synthesis (1995 Update)*, Portland, Oregon: Northwest Regional Educational Laboratory.

Creemers, B. P. M. (1994) *The Effective Classroom*, London: Cassell.

Fitz-Gibbon, C. T. (1992) 'School effects at 'A' Level – genesis of an information system', in D. Reynolds and P. Cuttance (eds), *School Effectiveness: Research, Policy and Practice*, London: Cassell.

Fullan, M. G. (1991) *The New Meaning of Educational Change*, New York: Teachers' College Press.

Fullan, M. G., Bennett, B. and Rolheiser Bennett, C. (1990) 'Linking classroom and school improvement', *Educational Leadership*, 47(8), 13–19.

Fullan, M. and Hargreaves, A. (1991) *What's Worth Fighting For: Working Together for your School*, Toronto: Ontario Public School Teachers Association.

Glickman, C. (1990) 'Pushing school reforms to a new edge: the seven ironies of school empowerment', *Phi Delta Kappan*, 68–75.

Gray, J., Reynolds, D., Fitz-Gibbon, C. and Jesson, D. (1996) *Merging Traditions: The Future of Research on School Effectiveness and School Improvement*, London: Cassell.

Hallinger, P. and Murphy, J. (1985) 'Assessing the instructional leadership behaviour of principals', *The Elementary School Journal*, 86(2), 217–48.

Hargreaves, A. (1992) 'Cultures of teaching: a focus for change', in A. Hargreaves and M. Fullan (eds), *Understanding Teacher Development*, London: Cassell.

Hargreaves, D. H. (1990) 'Accountability and school improvement in the work of LEA inspectorates: The rhetoric and beyond', *Journal of Education Policy*, 5(3), 230–9.

Hargreaves, D. H. (1995) 'School culture, school effectiveness and school improvement', *School Effectiveness and School Improvement*, 6(1), 23–46.

Hargreaves, D. H. and Hopkins, D. (1991) *The Empowered School: The Management and Practice of Developing Planning*, London: Cassell.

Hopkins, D. (1995) 'Towards effective school improvement', *School Effectiveness and School Improvement*, 6(3), 265–74.

Hopkins, D. (1996) 'Towards a theory for school improvement', in Gray, J., Reynolds, D., Fitz-Gibbon, C. and Jesson, D. (eds), *Merging Traditions. The Future of Research on School Effectiveness and School Improvement*, London: Cassell.

Hopkins, D. and Ainscow, M. (1993) *Making Sense of School Improvement: An Interim Account of the IQEA Project.* Paper presented to the ESRC Seminar Series on School Effectiveness and School Improvement, Sheffield.

Hopkins, D., Ainscow, M. and West, M. (1994) *School Improvement in an Era of Change,* London: Cassell.

Hopkins, D. and West, M. (1994) 'Teacher development and school improvement', in D. Welling (ed.), *Teachers as Leaders,* Indiana: Phi Delta Kappa.

Houtveen, A. A. M. and Osinga, N. (1995) *A Case of School Effectiveness: Organisation, Programme, Procedure and Evaluation Results of the Dutch National School Improvement Project.* Paper presented to the Eighth International Congress for School Effectiveness and Improvement, Leeuwarden.

ILEA (1986) *Primary School Development Plans: A Support Booklet,* Primary Management Studies, Inner London Education Authority.

Joyce, B. and Weil, M. (1995) *Models of Teaching* (5th edition), Englewood Cliffs, NJ: Prentice-Hall.

Joyce, B., Wolf, J. and Calhoun, E. (1993) *The Structure of School Improvement,* New York: Longman.

Louis, K. S. and Miles, M. B. (1990) *Improving the Urban High School: What Works and Why,* New York: Teachers' College Press.

McMahon, A., Bolam, R., Abbott, R. and Holly, P. (1984) *Guidelines for Review and Internal Development in Schools,* (Primary and Secondary School Handbooks), York: Longman/Schools Council.

Miles, M. B. and Ekholm, M. (1985) 'What is school improvement?', in W. van Velzen, M. B. Miles, M. Ekholm, V. Hameyer and D. Robin (eds), *Making School Improvement Work: A Conceptual Guide to Practice,* Leuven: OECD.

Mortimore, P., Sammons, P., Stoll, L., Lewis, D. and Ecob, R. (1988) *School Matters: The Junior Years,* Somerset, Open Books [Reprinted 1995 by Paul Chapman: London].

Myers, K. (ed.) (1995) *School Improvement in Practice: Schools Make a Difference Project,* London: Falmer Press.

Myers, K. and Stoll, L. (1993) 'Mapping the movement', *Education,* 182(3), 51.

OFSTED (1994) *Improving Schools,* London: HMSO.

Pocklington, K. (1995) 'The evaluator's view', in K. Myers (ed.), *School Improvement in Practice: Schools Make a Difference Project,* London: Falmer Press.

Reynolds, D., Creemers, B. P. M. and Peters, T. (eds) (1989) *School Effectiveness and Improvement: Proceedings of the First International Congress, London 1988,* Cardiff: University of Wales College of Cardiff; Groningen, RION.

Rosenholtz, S. J. (1989) *Teachers' Workplace: The Social Organisation of Schools,* New York: Longman.

Rutter, M., Maughan, B., Mortimore, P. and Ouston, J. (1979) *Fifteen Thousand Hours,* London: Open Books.

Sammons, P., Hillman, J. and Mortimore, P. (1995) *Key Characteristics of*

Effective Schools: A Review of School Effectiveness Research, London: Office for Standards in Education and Institute of Education.

Sarason, S. (1982) *The Culture of the School and the Problem of Change*, Boston: Allyn and Bacon.

Sizer, T. (1992) *Horace's School*, New York: Houghton Mifflin.

Stoll, L. (1992) *Making Schools Matter: Linking School Effectiveness and School Improvement in a Canadian School District*. Unpublished doctoral dissertation.

Stoll, L. and Fink, D. (1992) 'Effecting school change; the Halton approach', *School Effectiveness and Improvement*, 3(1), 19–41.

—— (1994) 'School effectiveness and school improvement: voices from the field', *School Effectiveness and School Improvement*, 5(2), 149–77.

—— (1996) *Changing Our Schools: Linking School Effectiveness and School Improvement*, Buckingham: Open University Press.

Stoll, L. and Thomson, M. (1996) 'Moving together: a partnership approach to improvement', in P. Earley, B. Fidler and J. Ouston (eds), *Improvement Through Inspection: Complementary Approaches to School Development*, London: David Fulton.

Stringfield, S. (1995) 'Attempting to enhance students' learning through innovative programs: the case for schools evolving into high reliability organisations', *School Effectiveness and School Improvement*, 6(1), 67–96.

Stringfield, S., Bedinger, S. and Herman, R. (1995) *Implementing a Private School Program in an Inner-City Public School: Processes, Effects and Implication from a Four Year Evaluation*. Paper presented at the ICSEI Congress in Leeuwarden, January.

Stringfield, S. and Slavin, R. (1991) 'Raising societal demands, high reliability organisations, school effectiveness, success for all, and a set of modest proposals', paper presented at the Interuniversitair Centrum Voor Onderwijsevaluatie, Twente.

Teddlie, C., Stringfield, S., Wimpelberg, R. and Kirby, P. (1989) 'Contextual differences in models for effective schooling in the USA', in B. P. M. Creemers, T. Peters and D. Hopkins (eds), *School Effectiveness and School Improvement: Proceedings of the Second International Congress, Rotterdam, 1989*, Amsterdam: Swets and Zeitlinger.

Thomas, S., Sammons, P. and Mortimore, P. (1995) 'Determining what adds value to student achievement', *Educational Leadership International*, 58(6), 19–22.

Velzen, W. van (1987) 'The International School Improvement Project', in D. Hopkins (ed.), *Improving the Quality of Schooling: Lessons from the OECD International School Improvement Project*, Lewes: Falmer Press.

Velzen, W. van, Miles, M., Ekholm, M., Hameyer, U. and Robin, D. (1985) *Making School Improvement work: A Conceptual Guide to Practice* Leuven: ACCO.

Wallace, R. et al. (1990) 'The Pittsburgh experience', in B. Joyce (ed.), *Changing School Culture Through Staff Development* (The 1990 ASCD Year Book), Alexandria, VA: ASCD.

Index